AMERICAN (m)avericks

EDITED BY SUSAN KEY AND LARRY ROTHE

PUBLISHED IN COOPERATION WITH
THE UNIVERSITY OF CALIFORNIA PRESS

The San Francisco Symphony
San Francisco, California

All inquiries about the sales and distribution of this volume
should be directed to the University of California Press.

University of California Press
Berkeley and Los Angeles, California

University of California Press, Ltd.
London, England

©2001 by The San Francisco Symphony

ISBN 0-520-23304-2

Cataloging-in-Publication Data is on file with the Library of Congress.

The paper used in this publication meets the minimum requirements
of ANSI / NISO Z390.48-1992 (R 1997) (*Permanence of Paper*).

Printed in Canada
Designed by i4 Design, Sausalito, California
Back cover: Detail from score of Earle Brown's *Cross Sections and Color Fields.*

10 09 08 07 06 05 04 03 02 01
10 9 8 7 6 5 4 3 2 1

TO PHYLLIS WATTIS—

FRIEND OF THE SAN FRANCISCO SYMPHONY,

CHAMPION OF NEW AND UNUSUAL MUSIC,

BENEFACTOR OF THE AMERICAN MAVERICKS FESTIVAL,

FREE SPIRIT, CATALYST, AND MUSE.

Contents

From the Editors

When Michael Tilson Thomas announced that he intended to devote three weeks in June 2000 to a survey of some of the 20th century's most radical American composers, those of us associated with the San Francisco Symphony held our breaths. The Symphony has never apologized for its commitment to new music, but American orchestras have to deal with economic realities. For the San Francisco Symphony, as for its siblings across the country, the guiding principle of programming has always been balance. It's what the box office demands. Twentieth-century radical American composers are not good box office. That is the conventional wisdom—at least it was until June 2000, when the American Mavericks festival reminded us that there is no conventional wisdom in art.

In ten concerts that attracted both long-time concertgoers and those who had never set foot in Davies Symphony Hall, the American Mavericks festival showcased twenty-two composers, all of them part of a tradition that is both notorious and elusive. In the following pages, we hope to introduce them as artists in their own right, and as members of a complex social and cultural system, a system that was not so much a movement as it is a state of mind. For if the mavericks have one thing in common, it is the almost naïvely pure belief that art can provide a key to the world. Twenty-two individual composers do not represent the entire spectrum of American maverick music, but we hope to give readers a better sense of both the circumstances that shaped this tradition and the creative visions that emerged from it.

Much of what follows may be familiar to audiences who attended the festival concerts, for the chapters dealing specifically with the maverick composers are based on program notes and essays written for the festival. We have recast these in an effort to illustrate and underscore the sweep of radical music in America, from the turn of one century to the turn of another. Those who authored the original notes and essays provided pointed and illuminating commentary on the music; here we have attempted to translate that commentary into an introductory history of the subject. We owe any success in this attempt to the authors, who gave us such good raw material; if we have missed the mark, we bear the responsibility. Two long-time observers of maverick American music, Alan Rich and Michael Broyles, have provided new introductions to the subject. Michael Tilson Thomas, a champion of this music since the beginning of his career, offers a concluding assessment.

The maverick approach to music-making makes extra demands on performers, and performers, more than any others, provide genuinely unique insights into the music: not as it exists on the page, but as a living process. To that end, we have incorporated San Francisco Symphony musicians' and guest artists' reactions to the music. We are grateful for their willingness to reflect on their experiences with this challenging—at times daunting—body of work.

The accompanying CD documents music from the festival to which readers would have little or no access, as well as commentary and discussion by Michael Tilson Thomas, composers, and other artists. Excerpts included on the CD are keyed into the text by this icon:

Without the support of Phyllis Wattis, a major supporter of the San Francisco Symphony for more than two decades, there would have been no American Mavericks festival—and no book such as this one, which is dedicated to her in recognition of her generosity and vision and spirit. At 94, she keeps exploring the world through art and supporting the art she loves. "I like strong music," she has said, "different, quirky music" and "anything with new twists in it." American Mavericks and Phyllis Wattis—the perfection of the match continues to amaze.

This book represents the collaboration of many colleagues, but our debt to some is so great that we must mention them here. San Francisco Symphony Executive Director Brent Assink is a long-time advocate of new music, and this book is his brainchild. Director of Artistic Planning Gregg Gleasner, who worked with Michael Tilson Thomas in creating the festival programming, supported us with his enthusiasm throughout this project. The CD included in this book would never have been produced without the assistance of John Kieser, Director of Operations and Electronic Media; Tom Hemphill and Linda Lukas, co-chairs of the San Francisco Symphony Players Committee; and Mary Proenza, who devoted hours to compiling excerpts into a finished disc. Renée Harcourt and Janet Mumford, the book's designers, transfigured raw words and images into art. Katherine Cummins, Managing Editor of the San Francisco Symphony's program book, provided the sharpest of copy-editing eyes and minds. Our greatest debt of gratitude is to Michael Tilson Thomas. In conceiving the American Mavericks festival, and in carrying it through so spectacularly against all expectations, he takes his place with the visionaries and pioneers (if not iconoclasts) whose work is celebrated in this book.

S.K.

L.R.

San Francisco, August 2001

Preface

BY LUKAS FOSS

What you will find in the following pages can help break down the stereotypes often connected to new music. Yes: All artists have to be mavericks and follow their own paths; they have to be obstinate, and have faith in the impossible, which is the creative process. As to stereotypes: We keep separating "emotional" and "intellectual," as if you have either one or the other. Wrong! You have to have both in the arts. The same applies to "serious" and "humorous." The more serious and daring the artist, the more you will find humor in the work. Without humor, the art is solemn, which is not serious enough. You find humor combined with tragedy in the great mavericks such as Shakespeare, Beckett, Kafka, Ives, and Cage. You also find an unending curiosity, a wish to keep learning. Goya, age 89, wrote: "I am still learning." That is the way I feel when I compose.

The wish to learn: that is one thing shared by all the composers whose stories fill this book.

Enjoy! Keep learning!

Lukas Foss

chapter one

THE AMERICAN MAVERICK TRADITION

BY ALAN RICH

"Music was born free, and to win freedom is its destiny." Ferruccio Busoni

As long as America has endured, there have been Mavericks in the land. Moses Maverick, of Netherlands ancestry, arrived in the New World on the *Mayflower*, with the new bride he had selected from among the fellow passengers. The Mavericks settled around Boston, where there is still a Maverick Square, which—by accident or design—happens to be a safe harbor for a cluster of small art galleries that preserve the maverick (lower case, this time) spirit.

That spirit seems to have been born, or at least named, some two centuries after the landing of the ancestral Mavericks. The descendant who cast the longest shadow, Samuel Augustus Maverick (1803–1870), linked his fate to the hundreds of kindred unfettered spirits of his time, rode westward from New England to seek his fortune, settled near San Antonio in the county that now bears his name, became a cattle rancher and, from the evidence, played a pretty good hand of poker. One day Sam Maverick won a herd of cattle in a poker game. For reasons still unclear, he decided not to brand them but to let them roam free on the open range—to become, as we use the term today, "mavericks."

Alan Rich's most recent book is *American Pioneers*

in the Phaidon Press 20th-Century Composers series.

One of the founders of the Bay Area station KPFA,

he moved on to become chief music critic for the

New York Herald Tribune and its still-thriving offspring,

New York magazine. He is currently classical music critic

for the *LA Weekly*.

That "open range" in Sam Maverick's time must have been a lively expanse, in more ways than just topographically. On these same wide-open spaces honored in poem and song, the American arts staked out their figurative claims. In a limitless terrain, extending coast-to-coast, free of artificial barriers—or, at least, any barriers that the willpower of American creativity couldn't overleap—the generations of free spirits that invented and then defined American uniqueness found their grazing land. Henry David Thoreau flourished on that range, in mind if not always in body. Walt Whitman gave it its yawp. Frederick Remington's canvases captured its color and its vastness. Its music was an eclectic mix. There were the hymns, dances, and folk tunes that had stowed away on the immigrants' ships from Europe and the slave ships from Africa, and which had flourished in America's bracing air.

But there was also more serious stuff. By 1842, say, the year the New York Philharmonic was founded, the masterworks of the great European composers—Handel, Haydn, Beethoven, Mendelssohn—were already established in major cities. New York had seen Mozart's *Don Giovanni* as early as 1826. As American cities grew and a culture-supporting aristocracy sought to emulate Europe's metropolitan amenities by building opera houses and concert halls, a certain cautious interest also developed around the possibility of implanting a made-in-America "serious" musical culture as well into this virgin and receptive American soil. The ideal for the up-and-coming American composer, it was widely felt, would be to emulate the great overseas masters.

By mid-century America's concert halls had begun to extend a cautious welcome to the first generations of American-born composers, their talents annealed and made safe in the European conservatories. Whatever their potential might have been for America's first "serious" composers to enrich their native land with a musical language comparable to Whitman's rough-hewn eloquence, a few years in the classrooms of Munich or Vienna converted them instead to creditable clones of Mendelssohn and Brahms, with an occasional pentatonic scale or tom-tom solo threaded into their orthodox symphonies and concertos to identify their exotic American-ness: John Knowles Paine, George Whitefield Chadwick, Edward MacDowell. One of the best of these fine retreads, the solid and substantial pedant Horatio Parker, joined the faculty of Yale University as professor of composition. There in his classroom, in the 1890s, he would have his nose continually tweaked by the most unmanageable of his students, Charles Ives.

A century later, we can still look back upon Ives to provide the purest definition of the American musical maverick. Think for a moment of what the musical equivalent of the branding iron, the indignity that Sam Maverick's herds had been so nobly spared, might entail. Music, as taught in the world's conservatories in Ives's time and practiced by history's most illustrious composers on both sides of the Atlantic, was a body of artistic creation manufactured according to known and respected rules. There was, for example, the sonata form, which dictated that

Charles Ives

Henry Cowell

John Cage

Lou Harrison

Sculptures by
Bruce Kueffer.

movements in an instrumental work begin and end in the same key, with the rate of contrast inside each movement dictated by an exquisite, immutable logic. The *Eroica* Symphony by that proto-maverick Ludwig van Beethoven demonstrated a certain freedom of spirit by running twice as long as anything before its time, but it still kowtowed to the sonata-form principle; so did the even-longer works, decades later, of Anton Bruckner.

One of Ives's famous run-ins with Horatio Parker came when Ives handed in the score of his First Symphony, which began in D major, wandered wildly through the whole spectrum of keys, and ended somewhere in the middle of next week. Parker was understandably aghast, Ives understandably rebellious. That once, Ives accepted a compromise. He recast his symphony—not a particularly rebellious work to today's ears, by the way—so that it emerged from its wanderlust in time for the demanded D-major ending. Not long afterward, his Yale diploma in hand and free from the Ivy League branding iron, Ives would compromise no more.

Inevitably, the more adventurous his compositions became, the longer they sat unplayed on his shelf. Given the tastes of concert audiences around, say, 1910—"old ladies of both sexes," Ives called them in his famously ill-tempered *Essays Before a Sonata*—it's easy to understand why a work that might involve three or four old-timey American folk songs played *simultaneously*, each with a different time-signature, might have encountered difficulties in building an enthusiastic following. It is axiomatic, among composers inspired to rebel against what music is supposed to sound like at a given time, that applause is slow in coming. A classic case: Ives's Second Symphony, composed in 1898, received its first performance, to a cheering New York Philharmonic audience, in 1951, with the old boy himself listening—not in a box at Carnegie Hall, but at home, on a table radio in his kitchen.

To Ives, with financial security assured by his other life as an insurance executive, getting his music heard was probably of less importance than maintaining his creative freedom. In reading through his voluminous essays on his own life in the world of music and his contempt for almost every other denizen of that world, you detect a certain relish in his accountings of the snubs and slights administered by the "old ladies" of the concert establishment. If you measure a composer's success by number of performances and extent of critical acceptance, life can be lonely for the committed maverick. Perhaps that doesn't matter; perhaps the soul-refreshment in the act of making music outweighs the ego-gratification in getting it heard. "Take away the records, and people will learn to sing," wrote a later, supremely ornery maverick, John Cage.

Strange to say, music's mavericks found little nourishing fodder on Sam Maverick's Texas prairie; breezes from an ocean—*any* ocean—were an important part of the mix. The westward Atlantic breezes brought in Europe's escapees: Edgard Varèse at first, then the Americans returning from their apprenticeships at Nadia's Boulangerie, then the astonishing new-music who's who fleeing Hitler's flames. The eastward breezes over the Pacific caught the ears of the West Coast rebels and wafted Cowell, Cage, and Harrison toward new musical languages from newly met Asian cultures. Under the urging of Varèse and his cohorts, New York's rebel forces grouped into activist cliques, put on concerts (of each other's own music, with themselves as principal audiences), and produced a short-lived but splendid magazine called, simply, *Modern Music*. The West Coast composers seemed content at first to work as loners; only later, with the growth of electronic-music labs in San Francisco, Stanford, and the remarkable California Institute of the Arts down south (founded, would you believe, by Walt Disney's millions!), did its composers tend toward common cause.

And Most Amazing of All—a Typical Symphonic Program of the Future

Last of a set of cartoons depicting "The World of Tomorrow in Music," from *Musical America*, February 10, 1939.

Tracing the bloodline of the American maverick, Cage falls into place in the third generation, begotten by Henry Cowell, whom Ives begat. Cowell's membership in the maverick herd dates from the day in 1912 when, at 15, he scandalized a San Francisco audience with a concert of his own piano music for fists and forearms no less than fingers. Later, he became one of the few to enjoy Ives's grudging confidence, arranged some of the few performances the old codger's music ever got during his lifetime, and ended up as his biographer. To the young Cage, Cowell served as mentor, encouraging him and his colleague-in-crime Lou Harrison in the creation of music for junkyard instruments, expanding their horizons with a consciousness of the cultural richnesses in the music of Asia and the Pacific Rim.

OK, so here's what we have as our profile as the American maverick. First, a contempt for the compositional rulebook as refined, redefined, and handed down by the European generations over, let's say, a millennium's span. Second, a willingness to expand the whole concept of musical sound to include resonant objects reclaimed from junkyards, empty packing boxes, pianos with bits of hardware imposed on their strings, and even, in one famous case, silence filled only with the ambient sounds of the surrounding space. Third, an increased receptivity to musics not traditionally regarded as "classical"—jazz, Third-World, ancient chant, whatever— and an interest in incorporating these resources into concert music branded with an American identity.

Far from defining a small rebellious faction of nut-case music-makers out on the far edge, "American maverick" now defines the vigorous growing tip of all music, fiercely independent and assured. Since the dawning of the electronic era, both as a tool for composers and as a way of affording them the dissemination that neither Ives nor his immediate "descendants" ever enjoyed, the very definition of what music is seems to change weekly. Borders disappear; American composers absorb the patterns of African drumming or Indonesian gamelan at the source, and return home to replicate them in music for symphony orchestra or for ad-hoc get-togethers. With portable tape machines and the phenomenal expanse of the compact-disc catalogue, access to today's (or, at least, yesterday's) music is a matter of a quick trip to a neighborhood record store or an even-closer dot-com.

The holdouts persist, of course. Composers as widely diverse as Elliott Carter and John Corigliano find plenty to say in music whose European ancestry is clear. Aaron Copland, in his time several kinds of maverick—in the jazz-drenched scores of the 1920s and in the folk song-infused ballets of the 1940s that are his best-known works—spent his last years experimenting with the European atonal practices advanced by Arnold Schoenberg.

In the years around World War II, when America's music schools offered refuge to some of the most influential standard-bearers of Europe's traditions—most notably Schoenberg and Ernst Krenek—many of America's young innovators sought out their teachings and found them wanting. Harrison and Cage came to Schoenberg at UCLA. Harrison actually turned out a few Schoenbergian pieces but then moved on to other, more vigorous, expressive modes. Cage and Schoenberg seem not to have hit it off at all; Schoenberg dismissed the young firebrand as "merely an inventor." Cage, speaking perhaps for American mavericks of his time, before his time, and after, took that as a compliment.

chapter two

THE MAVERICK AND THE PUBLIC

BY MICHAEL BROYLES

"Who *are* these guys?"

When Butch Cassidy asked the Sundance Kid that question, he was talking about their pursuers, a band of strangers as obsessed as they were mysterious. In another context, he could have been talking about 20th-century composers. Maverick composers have found us, or we've found them, transforming them from outlaws to heroes, from those who pursued an audience to those we seek out. We Americans have turned those composers into types that could thrive nowhere else.

The maverick tradition in this country's music is more than two hundred years old. But our fascination with the maverick really began in the 1920s. Before then, the maverick was mostly unknown and hidden away—as Charles Ives was hidden in an insurance office. The 18th-century composer William Billings was a maverick—not so much because of the hymns and songs and fuguing tunes he wrote, but simply because he wrote music and published a book of 120 original pieces, a feat that no other American composer of his time had approached. In the early 19th century, the Austrian immigrant Anthony Heinrich, working in a log cabin in Kentucky, began writing wild, bizarre, and for the time almost unplayable works. Billings and Heinrich achieved some brief popularity, but in those days Americans simply did not conceive of music as an art.

Michael Broyles's book *Mavericks and Other Traditions in American Music* is forthcoming from Yale University Press. With Denise Von Glahn he is also writing a biography of Leo Ornstein. His most recent book is *"Music of the Highest Class": Elitism and Populism in Antebellum Boston*. He is currently Distinguished Professor of Music and Professor of American History at The Pennsylvania State University.

Forward to 1921: Paul Rosenfeld, writer, critic, and champion of new music, surveyed the American music scene and found a bleak landscape. Looking ahead to the next twelve months in music, he anticipated a year like the previous one, which was like the one before that. He titled his morose observations "Prologue to the Annual Tragedy." Rosenfeld could have gone all the way back to the 1880s, because not much different had happened since then. Some radical composers, such as Charles Ives, Leo Ornstein, and Edgard Varèse, had come along, but the public remained skeptical.

Rosenfeld could not have known that the American music scene was about to undergo geologic change. Composers soon found ways to reach the public—not through the existing cultural structures, but by creating their own. They formed organizations that encompassed the entire gamut of the music world. They became impresarios, critics, and propagandists as well as artists. They turned the world of American music on its head. In doing so, they created for the American public the image of the artist as maverick.

Leo Ornstein, who began writing modernist, dissonant works around 1913, met with huge success, but as a performer, not as a composer. A fine pianist, Ornstein introduced musical modernism to America. Crowds flocked to his concerts, which featured much of his own music, but only to guffaw at what seemed to them a thoughtful, musical person gone berserk. Ornstein's pieces elicited shock, bewilderment, and amusement. Critics placed him on the lunatic fringe in American music. Ornstein did, however, make some inroads and create a small following, particularly among the literati, and this was crucial for what happened next.

Edgard Varèse arrived in America in 1915. Already a known radical in music, he was appalled that modernism was invisible on the American music landscape and determined to do something about it. In 1919, after a checkered career as a conductor, he somehow persuaded 125 wealthy New York patrons to back him, and he founded the New Symphony Orchestra, an organization dedicated to new music. Reaction to the first concert was so negative that the musicians refused to continue unless he leavened the programs with more traditional fare. Varèse would not compromise. Two weeks after the first concert, he resigned. The New Symphony Orchestra demonstrated that, for radical music to be accepted, a more radical approach was necessary.

Charles Ives's works never even got to the public. He had tried out some new pieces with professional musicians in the early 1900s, only to meet such negative reaction that he abandoned his efforts—retreating, but continuing to compose, until at last, in about 1920, he stopped writing music. Late in that decade, however, years after he had fallen silent, his work was discovered. Its discovery came as a result of a maverick paradox.

The paradox was this: Individual strengths could be appreciated only when individuals banded together, finding strength in numbers. The key to the mavericks' success—success as measured in increased public awareness—was self-organization, a principle on which the United States was built. But the mavericks made themselves heard not through individual efforts, but through communal labors. Mavericks such as Ives and Ornstein, who had tried to go it alone, had failed, and not even Varèse could overcome the hostility and conservatism of the American music scene.

But in 1922 Varèse tried again. He founded the International Composers Guild, the first of a new type of organization. Until Varèse disbanded it in 1928, the Guild presented three to four concerts each year of entirely new music. It was an immediate and continuing success, and it spawned other new-music organizations, particularly the League of Composers in New York (a spinoff resulting from tensions within the ICG), the Copland-Sessions Concerts, and the New Music Society, founded by Henry Cowell on the West Coast as a sister organization to the New York groups.

"The American Composer Must Sell His Product to the Small-Town Critic"

From *Musical America*, April 25, 1940.

How did the International Composers Guild, the League, and the New Music Society succeed when so many organizations before them (such as the New Symphony Orchestra) had foundered? The composers who formed the ICG, the LOC, and the NMS did what the literary modernists had done: They formed their own complete subculture. Rather than depend on the mainstream music world, they arranged their own concerts, put out their own publicity, and established music magazines that discussed the music and the concerts. They found champions and models among the many "little magazines" that were the bulwark of the literary avant-garde. Some modernist composers eventually became critics for major newspapers.

The ultramoderns of the 1920s were able to break out of the stasis that had characterized American music for at least forty years because they bypassed the prevailing music establishment. They never ignored the public; the public was invited on the mavericks' own terms. Audiences reacted at first with embarrassed laughter and some hissing, but the presenters persisted, sometimes lecturing listeners, sometimes repeating pieces. Composers had control of the concerts and could rearrange them to suit the situation. The public gradually began to respond, often filling the hall and dividing into groups of devotees and detractors.

American Folk Songs for Children IN HOME, SCHOOL AND NURSERY SCHOOL

A BOOK FOR CHILDREN,
PARENTS AND TEACHERS

by Ruth Crawford Seeger

ILLUSTRATED BY BARBARA COONEY

A ZEPHYR BOOK
Doubleday & Company, Inc., Garden City, New York.

Maverick composer Ruth Crawford Seeger became known
for her gentler endeavors.

The original individualist, maverick personality could flourish precisely because of this communal activity. With it, the American fascination with the artist-as-maverick began. In many ways the rebellious, funky rock musician of the 1960s (and on) is a manifestation of the avant-garde revolution of the 1920s. This lineage has encompassed the entirety of American music, both classical and popular, from John Cage to Frank Zappa.

While most traditional concert presenters and established critics looked askance at the performances of the new-music organizations, the upstart groups enjoyed pockets of support. Leopold Stokowski, Music Director of the Philadelphia Orchestra, premiered or programmed many ultra-modern composers in both Europe and America, including works by Schoenberg, Varèse, and Ornstein. Late in the 1920s, Nicolas Slonimsky put together avant-garde orchestral concerts, including some of the first public performances of Ives's music. Slonimsky also introduced American mavericks to European audiences. His efforts for new music had consequences, however. Because he was such an ardent champion, he never received the major conducting post that he deserved.

The Great Depression put an end to the musical experimentalism of the 1920s, and many of the more radical composers turned conservative. Seeing the economic suffering around them, some became advocates of leftist or socialist causes and sought to create more accessible music. Aaron Copland and Ruth Crawford Seeger turned away from dissonant, chromatic styles to embrace American folk music, while Henry Cowell sought to incorporate music from many cultures, especially Asia. Copland's fame in particular spread through his ballets of the 1930s and early '40s that drew heavily on folk sources, *Billy the Kid*, *Rodeo*, and *Appalachian Spring*.

Edgard Varèse and Carl Ruggles, who were not attracted to folk idioms, reacted differently. Each all but abandoned composition. And with both the public and their colleagues less interested in radical innovation, the organizations that supported it foundered. The League of Composers continued, but it was no longer the vital force it had been.

After World War II, a new group of radical, experimental composers emerged. These composers split into two streams, streams that were defined by New York City geography, Downtown and Uptown. Uptown composers found a home in academia—Princeton, Columbia,

ORCHESTRA AVOIDS "DEBATABLE MUSIC"

Philadelphia Programs to Consist Almost Wholly of Standard Works

PHILADELPHIA, Sept. 10.—"Debatable music" will be missing from the programs of the Philadelphia Orchestra in the coming season.

The Orchestra Association has made this decision, in its preliminary announcement to subscribers. "The programs will be devoted almost entirely to the acknowledged masterpieces. The directors feel in times such as the present, that audiences prefer music which they know and love and that the performance of debatable music should be postponed until a more suitable time. With these opinions the conductors fully concur." The orchestra has been notable in recent seasons for sponsoring extreme modernistic works.

Drastic economies have been made wherever possible, but owing to the fact that the income producing endowment funds are not bringing in as high a percentage as formerly, it has not been possible to reduce the price of tickets, even at a time of falling prices in most activities.

The season will run for thirty consecutive weeks, beginning Oct. 7-8-10. All the concerts will be given in the Academy of Music—an announcement which indicates that there will be none of the elaborate and expensive stage productions of recent years at the the Metropolitan Opera House.

Leopold Stokowski will start the season and will conduct seventeen weeks in all. He will, however, take only one long recess, from Jan. 13 to Feb. 27, when the conductor will be Issay Dobrowen, of the San Francisco Symphony Orchestra. Other conductors will be Alexander Smallens, Eugene Ormandy and Artur Rodzinski.

A new scenic setting has been devised according to the plans and suggestions of Leopold Stokowski for the Academy of Music stage. Not only will the scenery built for the orchestra provide a pleasant variation from the color background of the sets used in former seasons, but also it has the value of improving the acoustics.

In addition to the regular weekly series and the twelve Monday evening series of symphony concerts, there will be two series of Young People's Concerts of five each with Dr. Ernest Schelling as lecturer and conductor.

W. R. MURPHY.

The Depression affected the viability of maverick music. Above, an article from *Musical America*, September, 1932.

and Juilliard. Public performances centered on Carnegie Hall and later the new Juilliard-Lincoln Center complex, on the Upper West Side. Befitting their academic status, the Uptown composers' music was complex, dense, and intellectually challenging. It was frequently serial and atonal. Their academic connections gave them a platform to explain to the public what it was all about. Through academia, this branch of avant-garde mavericks became respectable. That these composers never engendered great public enthusiasm is an issue unto itself.

The real American mavericks had moved Downtown, particularly to Greenwich Village. John Cage, Morton Feldman, and the minimalists La Monte Young, Steve Reich, and Philip Glass lived and worked in and around the Village. For much of the 1950s, '60s, and '70s, the Uptown establishment, including its musicians, shied away from their music. Downtowners performed wherever they could, and, like their 1920s predecessors, they created their own venues.

Those venues varied, but they were seldom concert halls. Performances frequently took place in art museums. More often they were informal events in artists' lofts, arranged by the performers themselves and their friends. Many were multimedia affairs, encompassing music, dance, and a loose kind of theater, with visual spectacle running from experimental painting and sculpture to light shows. Well before she met John Lennon, Yoko Ono held multimedia events in her Soho loft.

In this mix, distinctions between the arts themselves seemed to break down, and the Downtown maverick composer made connections more often with artists in other fields than with other musicians. John Cage, Merce Cunningham, Robert Rauschenberg, and Jasper Johns often worked together. Fluxus, a radical group of wide-ranging conceptual-performance artists, took Cage as its guru and featured La Monte Young's music prominently. Cage himself said that his early concerts always attracted more artists than musicians. Later, composers such as Meredith Monk so mixed the various arts that the very term *composer* needed to be redefined.

When Philip Glass and Robert Wilson had the opportunity to present *Einstein on the Beach* at the Metropolitan Opera in 1976, it was an important symbolic event. Glass had made it Uptown—even though the Met took no financial risk, demanding that Glass and Wilson shoulder it all. After that, Uptown began to notice these Downtown mavericks.

But the going was still slow. The academic music world had successfully defined new music. Major orchestras, listening to their constituents, shied away from too heavy a dose. Two efforts were made to break the new-music barrier. When Pierre Boulez was appointed Music Director of the New York Philharmonic in 1971, he attempted to introduce contemporary music, both in regular programs and in special performances aimed at young people and called "rug concerts"—rugs replaced regular seating, and informality reigned. What was offered, however, was predominantly Boulez's own brand of serialism, and many mavericks still felt left out.

A broader effort occurred in Louisville. In 1953, after experiments in financing its own commissioning projects, the Louisville Orchestra received a major grant from the Rockefeller Foundation to commission forty-six new orchestral works each year, for four years. This initial grant spurred development of a comprehensive new-music program, and during the 1950s and '60s, the Louisville Orchestra introduced as many as four new pieces every Saturday afternoon. Works by more than 250 composers of all musical persuasions were recorded on the ensemble's First Edition Records label. Yet few of these made it into the repertory. Most were performed, recorded, and then archived.

The American maverick made no sudden breakthrough in the post-World War II world. Instead, boundaries between popular and classical, between Western and non-Western, between serious and playful music began to erode. Beginning with Cage, boundaries between the arts themselves seemed to dissolve. The notion of concert music as high art, abstract and a thing unto itself, was challenged by a new generation of composers and performing musicians who saw inspiration wherever it was found, and who drew upon that most American trait, experimentalism. A new generation of listeners came to table, raised on rock music, television, new art, and new kinds of film, open to any musical experience that proved interesting and exciting.

Once that happened, the maverick was everywhere.

chapter three

SEARCH FOR THE MODERN: Early 20th-Century Mavericks

CHARLES IVES

CARL RUGGLES

EDGARD VARÈSE

HENRY COWELL

RUTH CRAWFORD SEEGER

The maverick streak in American music broke out with an untamed vigor early in the 20th century, when America itself was beginning to assert its individuality and discover an identity apart from its European heritage. Both the music and the country owed much of their vigor to geographic and ethnic diversity, drawing from the established cultural centers of New England, from a massive tide of European immigration, and from the vibrant multi-culturalism of the West Coast. Connecticut's Charles Ives was East Coast Transcendental. Edgard Varèse was a Parisian who arrived in this country looking for new artistic freedoms. Henry Cowell, a native of the San Francisco Bay Area, grew up on a diet of sounds as Asian as they were European. Each of these composers uncovered a different vein of early American modernism in the society itself—raw material that entered the music and changed its sound: immediately, and also over the longer run of the century to come.

Composers from all three environments shared the compulsion to break away from existing musical norms and institutions. For these early modernists, a "maverick" stance involved challenging listeners and performers with works that were often difficult and dissonant—extreme in ways that went beyond Europeans of the same generation. Dissonance, in fact, acquired significance far beyond harmonic technique; composers found in it emotional, even spiritual, sustenance. "Modern" and "American" overlapped in intriguing ways, at times trapping composers between defiant rejection of centuries-long European traditions and contempt for the popular commercial sounds of their immediate environments. This aesthetic stance would later be challenged by their successors, but it established a fundamental benchmark against which those future mavericks would measure themselves.

CONTRIBUTORS TO THIS CHAPTER:
JAMES M. KELLER (IVES, VARÈSE,
AND COWELL), MICHAEL STEINBERG
(IVES, RUGGLES, AND COWELL), AND
SUSAN KEY (CRAWFORD SEEGER)

Pride of place in a lineup of American mavericks must go to New Englander Charles Ives, whom the *New York Times* critic Olin Downes, writing in 1924, described as "a composer who has not the slightest idea of self-ridicule and who dares to jump with feet and hands and a reckless somersault or two on his way to his destination." Ives was inspired, original, aggressive, untidy, hard-nosed, sentimental. He was enraged by the very existence of a genteel tradition of music-making. For him, "nice" was the ultimate putdown. He had absorbed these attitudes, as a child and an adolescent, in Danbury, Connecticut, from the great presence in his life, his father. George Edward Ives was Danbury's bandmaster, a music teacher, leader of theater orchestras, director of music at the Methodist church, and the only one of four siblings not to enter into a respectable life in commerce and industry. Paradoxically, Charlie was eventually to tread those paths of righteousness, when he became senior partner in the New York insurance firm of Ives & Myrick, where he made a fortune.

George Ives was not only a musician, he was an unsettlingly unconventional one, with an unbounded hunger for experimentation. He accompanied his family in C while they sang *Old Folks at Home* in E-flat, tried to teach them tunes in quarter-tones, played his cornet across the water to study the echo, worked with bells and glasses, and rigged up musical machines of his own invention. When his own band and another passed in the park, each playing a different march, he was delighted.

Not everyone took George Ives seriously. The handsome and athletic Charlie did. George, both in his lifetime and afterward, in memory, nurtured his son's fantasy and courage. Peter Burkholder has remarked that many of Ives's pieces "include the town or regimental band as a major actor in the pageantry." It is not only what the Danbury bands played—and Ives's music is always full of reference to hymns, marches, dance music, and other sounds from the vernacular—but their blending and colliding that determined the sound of his compositions. He loved musical collage and gave new meaning to the notion of polyphony. In his scores it is not just the counterpoint of individual musical strands but the coming together of whole different musics. He shocked his listeners by blurring the hallowed line between the cultivated and the popular. He questioned the idea that tempo should be stable and probed the possibility of flexible, evolving speeds. He found his way to polytonality, atonality, polyrhythms, and other devices that, like Leonardo's bicycle and contact lenses and ball bearings, all had to be reinvented by others. He even anticipated ideas dear to some composers in the 1960s: that any sound is potential music, that a stylistically neat and consistent articulation of musical materials is not a necessary part of the musical experience, and that a work need not be "fixed," but might be work-in-progress as long as its creator lived.

One of Ives's experiments in expanding the sonic palette resulted in a set of three pieces for two pianos tuned a quarter-tone apart, composed during 1923 and 1924. As did much of

Ives's music, the pieces underwent a long gestation; the second, *Allegro*, is derived almost entirely from piano compositions written a decade earlier. When all three were included in a program given in New York's Aeolian Hall in February of 1925, Ives explained: "These pieces were not presented as definitely completed works of art (or attempts at works of art). They were simply studies within the limited means we had with which to study quarter-tones." Pianist Julie Steinberg agrees. With Alan Feinberg, she played *Allegro* in the American Mavericks festival. Her experience on the second piano part convinced her that the pieces were "an interesting experiment, not an area with great potential as an extended technique." Having never played the work before, she was "surprised it wasn't more discombobulating," surmising that the quarter-tones

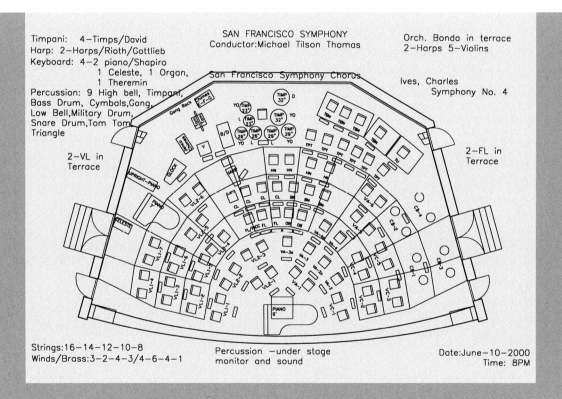

Stage setting diagram for Ives's Fourth Symphony, which calls for performers located at various points around the hall as well as a second conductor. Associate Conductor Alasdair Neale reflects on the unique perspective of hearing Ives "from within": "I had a small part to play in the proceedings myself. There are a few spots during the piece where the orchestra splits into two: which is to say that half of the orchestra goes at one tempo, and the other half at a completely different tempo. So ideally you really need two conductors to make it work. I ended up sitting right behind the podium—between the front stands of the second violins and violas—and I would spring to my feet to conduct these few sections of the piece with Michael Tilson Thomas. I guess you could call me a 'pop-up conductor.' Anyway, that only took place in the first two movements, so during the third movement I could just sit back and enjoy the performance from a rather unusual vantage point. Above all I'll never forget the climax of that third movement, as the chorus sang *Nearer, My God, to Thee* and the orchestra supported them in an extraordinarily beautiful pan-tonal wave of sound. I just sat back, closed my eyes, and let that amazing sonority wash over me." ▶

Charles Ives

(b. Danbury, Connecticut, October 20 1874; d. New York City, May 19 1954)

His formal education was at Yale, where he studied with Horatio Parker, but the most profound musical influence on his life came from his father, George Ives, a bandmaster bent on exploring music's expressive possibilities, with little regard for accepted notions of what made for good music. Charles played the organ and composed, but by the late 1890s he took a job at an insurance firm, and it was in the insurance business that he would make a fortune. He continued as a weekend composer, and among the large body of works he left are four symphonies—five, if you count the four-movement *New England Holidays*—as well as songs, choral works, and chamber music. Eventually it became clear that audiences were not ready for his musical experiments, and by the 1920s he stopped composing, though he continued to encourage a new generation of composers in their work, including Henry Cowell and Lou Harrison. He maintained his stance of contempt toward entrenched sensibilities even after the musical establishment began to discover and celebrate his worth.

LOU HARRISON ON THE GENEROSITY OF IVES: *"I was studying with Henry Cowell, and I wanted to know more about the music of Mr. Ives. So Henry said, "write to him!' and gave me the address. In a few weeks came this big crate of music. It was a mine, and I lived with it for ten years. I remember calling his New York brownstone once, because I wanted William Masselos, a brilliant pianist of his time, to do the first sonata, which I had had around for these ten years (you know, the crate!) and I had grown to love. I called the Ives residence and asked, 'Would it be all right? Mr. Masselos is really a first-class, grand-manner pianist, which is what this work needs.' Mrs. Ives said, 'Just a minute, I'll go up and talk to Mr. Ives.' And so upstairs she went. I waited on the phone, and she came down and said, 'Yes, it's fine.'"*

were more devices of color—tonal shadowing—than deeper structure: "Ives's piano technique might be described as 'classical' in its clarity of phrasing." Alan Feinberg, who played the first piano part, observes that the expansion of the twelve-note octave to twenty-four has a further effect: "doubling the pitch capacity and often forcing the two minds and twenty fingers that each control 88 keys to function as one, so that the melodies of each, which have only one-half of the material, will together add up to one: doubling the idea of what a piano can be."

What matters more than any of his inventions or discoveries is Ives's personal voice. Not every piece by Ives works, but at his best he is one of the most tender and amusing of song-writers and a genre painter whose sureness of touch is heart-piercing. Ives told Henry Cowell about his Second Symphony: "There is not much to say about the symphony. It expresses the musical feelings of the Connecticut country around here in the 1890s, the music of the country folk. It is full of the tunes they sang and played then...." "Not much to say" belies the skill with which Ives was beginning to find his signature ability to translate the "musical feelings" of an environment now far removed from most listeners into universal human feelings.

Ives's belief in the power of music to speak to the most central questions of human existence also led him to awesome grandeur of utterance, as in the Symphony No. 4, in which he literally and figuratively pulled out all the stops. In addition to a full raft of keyboard instruments, including organ, the ensemble includes a group of harps and violins, in positions above the main orchestra, that Ives characterized as either the Star of Bethlehem or Halley's comet, depending on the listener's spiritual persuasion—"a sign in the sky," as Michael Tilson Thomas explains, also pointing to a subterranean percussion ensemble in the last movement whose long rhythmic cycles represent "the universal clock ticking in its inexorable way; so we are pulled between the sky and the earth." For the individual performers in this massive ensemble, each part maintains its autonomy, collectively creating, in the words of solo pianist Michael Linville, "the face of Ives that peers through the many layers of orchestral fabric." The sum total of such layering is, says orchestral pianist Peter Grunberg, "a phantasmagorical world: half narrative, half abstract."

Carl Ruggles is often mentioned together with his slightly older friend Charles Ives. The two make about as unconvincing a couple as Bach and Handel or Haydn and Mozart. They share what used to be called, with admiration, Yankee individualism, and both were uncompromising figures, as disdainful of the "mainstream" as it was of them. Ives discovered in himself a genius for life insurance comparable to his genius for music, and it made him a prosperous man who could protect his tender artistic ego by pretending that composing was an eccentric's hobby. Ruggles scraped together an irregular sort of living from playing the violin, engraving, teaching,

Carl Ruggles

(b. East Marion, Massachusetts, March 11 1876; d. Bennington, Vermont, October 24 1971)

MICHAEL TILSON THOMAS: *"As did many people in that generation, Ives and Ruggles had a conception of dissonance. For them, dissonance had kind of a challenging quality that they wished to embrace. They wanted to change the perception of dissonance as something ugly or painful, and transform it into something affirmative and ecstatic. That was a major part of what Ruggles and the earlier generation of modernists wanted to do."*

He began violin lessons when he was 6 and was a musician ever after, going on to write music criticism, teach, and compose. He kept company with Ives, Cowell, and Varèse, but his music has an individuality that defies comparison. He was a man of craggy voice and craggy temperament. He wrote a small body of music—only eight published compositions—but what he left aims high, reaching for honesty and spiritual exaltation. In later life he turned to painting as his primary creative outlet. His work was neglected almost until his death, when Michael Tilson Thomas was in the forefront of a Ruggles rediscovery.

conducting, and private patronage. Like his European contemporary Arnold Schoenberg, he was an able painter. Henry Cowell summed him up: "...irascible, lovable, honest, sturdy, original, slow-thinking, deeply emotional, self-assured, and intelligent."

Ruggles and Ives were radically different as artists, and Wilfrid Mellers has summed up their differences:

> The eclecticism of Ives's technique—his simultaneous use of modal, diatonic, and chromatic materials from multifarious aspects of the past and present—is part of his immediacy, his awareness of environment. Ruggles, on the other hand, is neither eclectic nor profuse. In a long life he has written— and rewritten, again and again—only a handful of works; and they are in a style as consistent as Ives's music is protean and inconsistent. This style is comparable with, and related to, one aspect only of Ives's music: the freely evolving, non-tonal polyphony in which he expressed both his freedom from the past and his desire for identity with Nature. From Ruggles's music all those tune-filled, rhythm-dominated, harmonically- ordered conventions which approximate to the values of Society are rigorously banished. His is a dedicated art; and it is dedicated to the integrity of his own spirit.

Ruggles was an able visual artist. Here is an example of one of his "vertical sonorities" as rendered in a painting.

Ruggles has none of Ives's folksiness and occasional senti- mentality, he is not a quoter or collage artist. He left a catalogue so small as to make Anton Webern seem prodigal by comparison, a catalogue of pieces endlessly fussed over and brought as near to perfection as he knew how. Ruggles's small output and stubborn iconoclasm obscure his aesthetic kinship with 19th-century Romanticism, evident both in his grand compositional gestures and his quest for meaning in music. "In all works," he said, "there should be the quality we call mysticism. All the great composers have it." Perhaps also in this tradition is his tendency to turn to visual and poetic imagery for inspiration, as in his best-known work, *Sun-treader*, whose title comes from Robert Browning's "Pauline": "Sun Treader, Light and Life be thine forever." Listening to the work, one would never guess that its source is a line from the English poet. Ruggles's massed chords, uncompromising dissonance, and often brash orchestration suggest a rugged American landscape far from the gentle effusions of Browning's first published poem.

Sun-treader, like most of Ruggles's music, was rarely performed until the last years of his life. It was admired by colleagues like Ives and Varèse; more often it met with incomprehension and hostility. Indeed, the music's confrontational quality still offers challenges—and rewards—for performers as well as listeners. San Francisco Symphony violinist Darlene Gray mused on her experience playing *Sun-treader*:

> *The reactions I had to the Ruggles were all emotional reactions, and I was startled by them. Music like this is really not my thing, but when we played it, I thought it was stunning. Before the performance, I had been gritting my teeth, wishing I could play with earplugs, and counting madly.*

Carl Ruggles in "the little schoolhouse" where he lived. The photo dates from 1970, around the time Michael Tilson Thomas met the composer.

> *Then I remember the first chords: they glittered for me. Every note rang in my being. I could hardly believe I was feeling this way about music by Carl Ruggles! And then the audience whooped and hollered, and I know they heard what I did.*

Michael Tilson Thomas met Ruggles in 1970, when he first conducted the composer's works. He recalls "huge polyphonic structures written out in very large notes on wrapping paper on the walls of the little schoolhouse where he lived. Then he would give these pieces what he called 'the test of time': he would play every vertical sonority, every chord, on the piano: once, twice, ten, twenty, fifty, perhaps hundreds of times, as loud as he could, because, as he said to me: 'I thought that if I could still stand the sound of that damn thing after a hundred times or so it would sound pretty good a couple of hundred years from now!'"

If Ives drew his unconventionality directly from his upbringing, nothing in Edgard Varèse's early life suggested the pioneering route he would travel. His musical training reads like a résumé for any number of properly trained French musicians at the turn of the century: study at the conservative Schola Cantorum with Albert Roussel (in composition, counterpoint, and fugue), Charles Bordes (early music, which remained an abiding passion of Varèse's), and

Vincent d'Indy (conducting) before transferring to the Paris Conservatory to hone his skills as a composer under the eminent organist Charles-Marie Widor. In 1907, however, Varèse left Paris for Berlin, where he fell under the spell of the visionary Ferruccio Busoni and eagerly followed the developments of Schoenberg. He returned to Paris in 1913 and started hanging out with Apollinaire, Satie, and Cocteau, as well as with the futurist noise-theorist Luigi Russolo. He was called for military service at the outbreak of World War I but was promptly released due to a lung ailment.

It seemed a propitious moment to leave Europe, and on December 18, 1915, Varèse sailed for New York, where he arrived eleven days later. By that time his oeuvre included a couple of Strauss-sized symphonic poems (one of which, *Bourgogne*, had earned him rough treatment from the Berlin critics but encouragement from Debussy) and an incomplete opera, on the Oedipus myth, to a libretto by Hugo von Hofmannsthal. He had left most of his early manuscripts in Berlin, where they disappeared in a fire of mysterious origin; he personally destroyed *Bourgogne* a few years before his death. Apart from one early song (to a text by

Varèse was part of a circle of avant-garde artists working in diverse media. This photo of the maverick composer is by the maverick photographer Man Ray.

Verlaine), Varèse's catalogue comprises thirteen works, all of which date from his full maturity. (These have been eked out by a couple of reconstructions and completions by helpful followers.)

Amériques, the gigantic orchestral work begun in 1918 and described by the composer as "a meditation, the impression of a stranger who asks himself about the extraordinary possibilities of our civilization," marks Varèse's rupture from the mainstream of European tradition and the beginning of his idiosyncratic modernism. Yet for a performer, the experience confirms modernism's encounter with—and debt to—primitivism. Sitting close to the percussion section in a performance during the American Mavericks festival, pianist Peter Grunberg was struck by the intense physicality of the work. Percussionist Jack Van Geem agrees: "It's surprising what a primal expression of pulse and rhythm *Amériques*

became. The more intimate we became with it, the more it fixed something in our primal rhythm center. It's a 'fussy' piece, but the net result is this very urgent rhythmic experience."

The years after *Amériques* were marked by Varèse's frustrating search for instruments that would expand the boundaries of musical sound. In a series of lectures given in 1936 in Santa Fe, Varèse laid out his aesthetic vision; a reporter for the *Santa Fe New Mexican* described "the future which Varèse sees with the intensity of a prophet, which he has anticipated with

Edgard Varèse

(b. Paris, France, December 22 1883; d. New York City, November 6 1965)

He studied with Albert Roussel and Vincent d'Indy, but his music sounds nothing like theirs. Early in his career he had to sell pianos to support himself, and once he played a minor role in a John Barrymore silent film. In 1915, when he arrived in the United States, he poured his energies into the cause of new music, founding the International Composers Guild and organizing performances of works by such composers as Stravinsky, Schoenberg, Ruggles, and Cowell. For him, sound itself was an organizing principle, and his works are like sonic sculptures. Sirens scream, huge blocks of noise collide, rhythms cross and crisscross. He anticipated the creative possibilities of electric-instrument research, even ceasing composition for a time because the technical means were not yet available to realize his aesthetic vision.

emphasis on noise in his ultramodern symphonies. Between 'noise and sound' he finds no difference for 'noise is sound in the making.' When asked 'Are you a musician?' his reply is 'No, I am a worker in rhythm, frequencies and intensities.'" At the time he gave these lectures he was working on a composition for radio, to be entitled *Espace* and to be broadcast simultaneously from points around the globe. *Espace* was never completed, and Varèse ceased composing for nearly two decades, only resuming after the development of electronic composition. In 1962 he stated that "Our new medium has brought to composers almost endless possibilities of expression, and opened up for them the whole mysterious world of sound."

If you ask the average music lover to name the most influential "classical" composers of the 20th century, you are likely to receive a reply that includes (but that may not exceed) Debussy, Schoenberg, Stravinsky, and Bartók. Ives and Webern might surface on a few lists, and possibly Boulez, but not one in fifty is likely to cite Varèse. To a large extent, Varèse is the overlooked pioneer of modern music—overlooked, perhaps, because his influence was not widely felt until long after his pieces were written, and (when it finally was) his most profound lessons were picked up by composers of electronic music, which many listeners viewed with defensive suspicion. "There is no avant-garde," Varèse observed, "only some people a bit behind." Varèse was that lucky artist who was both a visionary and a pioneer; he both imagined, and later realized, the potential of new sound—an achievement that John Cage recognized when he paid tribute to Varèse as the one who "fathered forth noise into 20th-century music."

At the turn of the century, California was teeming with noises of all kinds. Henry Cowell's Bay Area upbringing freed him from the assumption that all worthwhile culture came from the other side of the Atlantic. Nearby San Francisco was full of Asian music, and to the end of his life, Cowell's musical fantasy was more and more drawn to sounds from across the Pacific. His father, a failed fruit farmer from Ireland by way of British Columbia, and his mother, a writer from Midwestern farming stock, called themselves "philosophical anarchists" and allowed their son the most wide-ranging and improvised of educations. He explored the piano by himself, tried his hand at inventing new pieces, absorbed whatever was in the air in San Francisco's Chinese and Japanese neighborhoods, developed a deep love of Irish folk music, and came to include in his concept of "music" virtually all sounds put into the air by nature and human beings. Virgil Thomson noted that "the variety of [Henry Cowell's] sources and composing methods is probably the broadest in our time."

At 17 he met his first real teacher, the remarkable Charles Seeger. Seeger, the freest of free spirits, was one of the first classically trained musicians (a Harvard graduate and at 24 an opera conductor in Germany) to accept non-Western music as no less interesting than European.

Henry Cowell

(b. Menlo Park, California, March 11 1897; d. Shady, New York, December 10 1965)

Growing up near San Francisco and absorbing a wealth of music that came from across the Pacific, he was among the first to embrace the idea that "serious" music can exist outside the Western tradition. He absorbed all influences, from Eastern to American folk to European classical. He invented the "tone cluster"—in which a piano is played not just by fingers, but by forearms and fists. In the 1920s he created a sensation with his music in Europe. On his return to this country he founded the quarterly journal *New Music*, taught, and composed prolifically. His 1936 arrest on a morals charge led to nearly four years' imprisonment in San Quentin, yet even under these circumstances he remained active in the composition and promotion of new music—and established a prison music-education program. He was a great champion of Ives and with his wife wrote the first important study of that composer, *Charles Ives and His Music* (1955). He served as music editor of the Office of War Information in World War II, and in 1956 he embarked upon a State Department tour in which he explored the music of many lands.

From the score of Cowell's Piano Concerto. The extended note ranges are to be played with the forearm.

Cowell found himself nicely in tune with him. He even allowed Seeger to persuade him that a little formal training in harmony and counterpoint would help give clearer form to his ideas.

After military service at the end of World War I, Cowell plunged into international music traffic with characteristic vigor. He gave a recital in New York, toured Europe five times in ten years, was the first American musician to visit the Soviet Union, made useful contact with publishers, played for Schoenberg's composition class in Berlin, and met Bartók, who introduced him to Falla, Ravel, and Roussel. He had already written an extraordinary book titled *New Musical Resources*, in which he formulated fresh ideas on harmony, rhythm, acoustics, and notation.

Like Charles Ives before him, Cowell came to the study of music with ears wide open, and by the time he was 13 he was already composing pieces that employed one of the devices for which he is widely remembered: the tone cluster. Tone clusters are essentially chords that comprise notes that reside in close proximity to each other. Where the chords of traditional harmony are made of notes separated by intervals of pitch, tone clusters use groups of contiguous notes, which traditional harmony classifies as dissonant to one another. In 1913, at an event sponsored by the San Francisco Musical Society at the Saint Francis Hotel, Cowell went a step further by unveiling to amazed listeners a further pianistic development: altering the instrument's tones by inserting objects on the piano's strings and by plucking or strumming directly on the strings with his hands, dispensing with the intermediary of the keyboard.

In the hierarchy of musical instruments, the piano was (and still is) placed on a pedestal by many listeners. Monkeying about with its strings or extracting sounds from it in any non-traditional way were therefore considered by many to be musical sacrilege. It took a while for Cowell's sound-world to catch on, and, until it did, critics bound to uphold traditional values had a field day. Warren Storey Smith, writing in the March 12, 1929 edition of the Boston *Post*, reported to his readers (in an article irresistibly titled "Uses Egg to Show Off the Piano"): "Henry Cowell, in the suite for what he is pleased to term 'solo string and percussion piano' with chamber orchestra, has added to *materia musica* a darning-egg and a pencil, with which, together with more familiar implements, he assailed the innards of a grand piano.... Many of the sounds which Mr. Cowell achieved last evening might be duplicated with a tack-hammer and any convenient bit of unupholstered furniture." And from across the seas, Paul Zschorlich observed, in Berlin's *Deutsche Zeitung* of March 13, 1932, "It is said about Cowell that he has invented tonal groups that can be played on the piano with the aid of fists and forearms! Why so coy? With one's behind one can cover many more notes! The musical inmates of a madhouse seem to have held a rendezvous on this occasion."

Such procedures were certainly still outré when Cowell first played his Piano Concerto. He actually unleashed the piece on the public gradually, playing one movement — or possibly two — with the Conductorless Orchestra in New York before mounting a complete performance in December 1930, with the Havana Philharmonic. The piece is great fun, but it has gone almost unplayed since its premiere; it waited until 1978 for its first full performance in the United States. The concerto's three movements — "Polyharmony," "Tone Cluster," and "Counter Rhythm" — together last only about seventeen minutes, and they're full of tonal, rhythmic, and (after a fashion) melodic variety. The solo part cannot be negotiated successfully by a pianist whose idea of technique is defined by Hanon and Czerny exercises, as quite a lot of the playing involves attacking the piano with the forearms rather than with the fingers. It may look — and sound — like pretty wild stuff, but Cowell actually plumbs the harmonic implications of competing clusters with considerable sophistication, and the pianist is challenged to figure out how to enliven Cowell's score by combining fidelity to the notation with sensitive voicing and phrasing.

All his life, this composer of about a thousand pieces was more

A young Henry Cowell demonstrates his unconventional approach to the piano.

Pianist Ursula Oppens throws herself into Henry Cowell's music. "Although I had known much of the solo piano and chamber music of this great innovator," she says, "I was unprepared for the incredible richness of the combined sounds of the orchestra together with the piano clusters, as well as for the sheer fun of playing the concerto."

than just a composer. Kyle Gann explains:

> He came into a world not nearly prepared for his far-reaching musical vision, and he realized that, to bring that vision about, it was not enough to simply compose the music. He had to prepare the ground, start a new foundation; rethink the materials, provide the theory, provoke the public into listening, sift through and comment upon the music of his time, champion composers who were on the right track, arrange their concerts, publish their scores, and explain exotic musics of the world in such a way that would put new music in context.

A Guggenheim Fellowship took Cowell to Berlin for study of comparative musicology. Four years later saw the beginning of an unfortunate interlude in his life, when in 1936 he was convicted of a charge of homosexual conduct and sentenced to time in San Quentin. The efforts of fellow composers secured his release in 1940 (he was pardoned in 1943 by the governor of California), and as evidence, perhaps, that his reputation had been rehabilitated even in the eyes of so determined a guardian of public morality as the United States government, he was the Office of War Information's resident expert on Asian music during World War II. He edited the much-imitated symposium *American Composers on American Music*, and with his wife, Sidney Robertson Cowell, he wrote *Charles Ives and His Music*, the first book on that great pioneer. He founded and edited the quarterly *New Music* and found time to teach at the University of California in Berkeley, and at Stanford, Mills, Bennington, Columbia, the Peabody Conservatory, and the New School for Social Research. Among those who learned from him were John Cage, George Gershwin, and Burt Bacharach. Gann states it simply: "It is not difficult to argue that Cowell was the least tradition-bound, most original musical thinker and theorist of his era."

The modernist cultural milieu in which Ives, Ruggles, Varèse, and Cowell worked had not thrown off all the social prejudices of an earlier era, as evidenced by a deep-seated misogyny. Not just composers, but many educators and critics deplored the feminization of American culture. The rhetoric of the 'teens and 'twenties is full of evidence: Charles Ives asserting that "a good dissonance is like a man," the 1922 Music Teachers National Association Proceedings sounding an alarm about "the feminization of music," a 1919 review of a concert of American music sneering at "effeminate" elements in music, ten years later the journal *Modern Music* citing as a hopeful sign "a distinguishing virility" in American modernist composers.

Even so, a woman emerged from this atmosphere with one of music history's most original compositional voices. Ruth Crawford Seeger studied in Chicago with Adolf Weidig; among the prominent figures who influenced her during her early years were Dane Rudhyar, Carl Sandburg, and Henry Cowell. After spending the summer of 1929 at the MacDowell Colony, she went to New York City under the patronage of Blanche Walton, where her circle included Cowell, Rudhyar, and Varèse. She also began a lifelong friendship with Carl Ruggles. ("Carl Ruggles swears in every sentence he speaks," she said, "and makes an art of telling worse stories than any one else dares tell. But his music soars in rarefied atmosphere.")

While in New York, Cowell arranged for her to study composition with his own mentor Charles Seeger. Seeger was at first reluctant to take on a woman student but was immediately impressed by her skills and dedication (though he was not above excluding her from serious gatherings of his male colleagues). Perhaps it is not surprising, given her environment, that Crawford would eschew any musical qualities identified as feminine (lyrical melodies, consonant harmonies, gently flowing rhythms) and turn instead to strict, systematic procedures based on her teacher's (and, later, husband's) theories of modern composition. Using Seeger's theory of

Ruth Crawford Seeger with her husband, Charles, and their children, Mike and Peggy, about 1937.

"dissonant counterpoint," she created a body of work notable for its ingenious formal procedures and concentrated vocabulary.

Crawford Seeger's String Quartet of 1931 is her best-known work. The Andante movement is often played on its own, either in its original quartet form or arranged for string orchestra. The movement is based on the novel idea of using dynamics as a structural element rather than an expressive decoration. The instruments form clusters—their lines differentiated by varying dynamic sequences—that arc from a subdued low point to a climax. As her biographer Judith Tick notes, the technique creates a remarkable blend of melody, texture, and dynamics: "Accumulating tension like a spring that is stretched ever tauter, when the upper climax is reached and the texture releases into a welcome homophony of articulation, what follows is a rebounding explosive energy."

After Crawford married Charles Seeger, she shared his rejection of fine-art music in favor of folk music as an extension of political views stimulated by the Depression. They were far from alone in this evolution; Aaron Copland is only the most-cited modernist whose ideologies led to an aesthetic turnabout. For Crawford Seeger, the turnabout meant abandonment of composition altogether; only at the end of her life did she contemplate writing concert music again. Thus, within a brief span, she would explore, refine, and give up a promising career in modern composition to devote herself to musical Americana, education, and family life.

As did her friend Carl Ruggles, Crawford found inspiration in other art forms. A gifted poet, she once penned the poignant line, "spirit of me/Dear rollicking far-gazing straddler of two worlds." In a sense, of course, every American composer is a "straddler of two worlds," manipulating an Old World artistic heritage in a New World environment. Both the life and music of Crawford Seeger, however, are full of contradictions that offer no convenient synthesis. A woman mastering a man's idiom—as modern composition was in the 1920s—a poet wielding a musician's language, and a keen intellect probing an unconscious tradition: artistic and personal dichotomies define the life and legacy of Ruth Crawford Seeger.

As disparate as their personal lives and musical styles were, these early mavericks shared a faith in the potential of music to speak from the heart and to evoke individual visions. They may have been cynical about the musical establishment, or about the received wisdom of compositional rules, but they were unashamedly committed to their art. And while they may have rebelled against musical techniques of the past, they were not without a deep love of their predecessors. To their successors they bequeathed less a particular approach to composition than an example: of courage and confidence in the face of hostile critics and audiences, and—through a body of work that begs to be described by that hackneyed but here appropriate term "unique"—an example of what could result from the belief in music's power to communicate a fiercely personal engagement with the world.

Ruth Crawford Seeger

(b. East Liverpool, Ohio, July 3 1901; d. Chevy Chase, Maryland, November 18 1953)

In her lifetime she was known mainly as a compiler of American folk songs, but Ruth Crawford was a remarkable composer in her own right. She pursued studies of piano and composition at the American Conservatory in Chicago, later studying composition in New York with Charles Seeger. She composed on a level with the finest of her contemporaries, becoming the first woman composer to receive a Guggenheim Fellowship in 1930, which she used for further study in Berlin and Paris. After her marriage to Seeger in 1931, she turned increasingly away from writing music to the more populist pursuits with which she became identified.

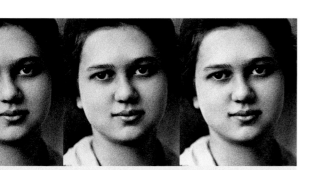

MICHAEL TILSON THOMAS: *"There's a whole interesting story to be written about people who were radical composers involved with dissonant or experimental musical language in the '30s and who became much more concerned with work in ethnomusicology, …which was partially an aesthetic but partially a political decision. There were many different sides of what radicalism as a musician meant. Did it mean being radical in the notes, or did it mean being radical in your social, or political, or other kinds of activities? That's an ongoing question."*

chapter four

FINDING AN AMERICAN SOUND: Two Contemporaries

DUKE ELLINGTON
AARON COPLAND

As a relative latecomer to nationhood, and as a nation based more on abstract principle than historical associations or ethnicity, the United States offers no ready marker of national identity. As a result, Americans from the earliest days of the republic have tried to define the American identity—and American artists' have been some of the most compelling voices in this dialogue. Yet the same factors that have made American musical culture the most vibrant in the world have placed its musicians in a double bind. The sounds that have come to be identified as "American" have come from class and ethnic sources outside the mainstream of "high culture." Thus popular musicians struggle to be taken seriously, and serious composers struggle to reconcile the genres, techniques, and resources of a European-developed art with their native popular music. Since the beginning of the 20th century, urbanization and the mass media have both confused and enriched the issue.

Duke Ellington and Aaron Copland, celebrated contributors to this cultural dialogue, have more in common than the proximity of their births. Both were from minority groups. Both enjoyed success within established institutional frameworks and created accessible, easily digestible music that raised questions about their status as mavericks. Both responded to the new audiences created by radio, phonograph, and film. Both wrestled with the tension between their individual creative visions and audience expectations, ultimately creating styles at once personal and unmistakably American.

CONTRIBUTORS TO THIS CHAPTER:
GROVER SALES (ELLINGTON) AND
MICHAEL STEINBERG (COPLAND)

A century after Duke Ellington's birth, the fascination with the man and his music looms immeasurably larger than it did during the nearly fifty years of his astonishing creativity. In the heyday of the Swing Era of the '30s and '40s, Ellington enjoyed public repute mainly as a writer of song hits and leader of one of hundreds of dance bands, though hardly in the rarefied strata of income and widespread popularity of Benny Goodman, Artie Shaw, and Glenn Miller. Author of more than two thousand compositions, he enriched the jazz lexicon with its first true concertos, its first extended works, its first use of a wordless human voice as an orchestral instrument, and, most of all, his transformation of the music of the dance hall and the cabaret into the realm of timeless art.

A late bloomer compared to two other jazz icons of his era, Louis Armstrong and Fats Waller, Ellington was born in 1899 in Washington DC to a cultivated family that showered him with the unstinting love and protection worthy of an ideal Freudian upbringing. "I was spoiled rotten by all the women in my family," he recalled. Marked as a special child, he was started on piano at 7 and soon developed the ducal poise that early on earned him his nickname. After a false career move as a painter, he became smitten with ragtime and the kings of Harlem "stride" piano, James P. Johnson and Willie "The Lion" Smith, who left a lifelong impress on his compositional and piano style. He picked up pointers in harmony and arranging from the prestigious black musicians Doc Perry, Henry Grant, and Will Vodery, the staff arranger for the Ziegfeld Follies.

After gigging around Washington with a small combo, Ellington made the inevitable move to New York to front a six-piece band at Harlem's seedy Kentucky Club. In 1927, he began a five-year engagement at the lavish, mob-owned Cotton Club—a period that left a definitive mark on his career. In addition to playing music for dancing, Ellington faced the workaday challenge of providing background scores for the exotic and provocative floor shows that the canny management staged during the "Harlem Renaissance" to reinforce and cater to lurid stereotypes nourished by many white patrons, stereotypes of primitive jungle rites and sexually uninhibited blacks. In contrast to Fletcher Henderson, Don Redman, and Jimmie Lunceford, whose bands played exclusively for dancers, Ellington was thrust into the arena of composing a series of impressionist tone poems rooted in the blues, and he reworked and enriched this music continually for the next forty years: *Creole Love Call, The*

Duke Ellington corrects a score.

Mooche, Black and Tan Fantasy. Just as Béla Bártok rarely strayed from the folk music of his native Hungary, Ellington never abandoned the gold mine of folk blues.

What critics were beginning to call the "Ellington effect" arose from Ellington's collaboration with some amazing musicians. Foremost was trumpeter and co-composer Bubber Miley, whose toilet-plunger mute evoked plaintive sobbings and terror-ridden screams. By the early 1930s, Ellington filled his band with a wealth of distinctive improvising soloists: alto saxophonist Johnny Hodges, the dominant voice on the instrument until the advent of Charlie Parker in the '40s; trumpeter Cootie Williams, who mastered the plunger's art under the guidance of Joseph "Tricky Sam" Nanton; and Nanton himself, a sorcerer who used the plumber's friend to make the trombone a human voice crying in anguish, laughing obscenely, or growling in anger. The grand tradition of New Orleans clarinet virtuosity lived on in Barney Bigard, whose limpid bluesy reed fluttered like a crazy flag above the stomping ensemble charged by the big-toned boom of Wellman Braud's bass. Juan Tizol, the Puerto Rican trombonist-composer, made essential contributions to the band's standards, including *Caravan* and *Perdido.* Harry Carney was the first to coax jazz from the cumbersome baritone sax and remained anchorman of the reed section for four decades. Longtime tenures with Ellington were the rule rather than the exception in a business where sidemen in bands were wont to change shop frequently and with breathtaking dispatch. "Everyone in the band knew we were working with a genius," said clarinetist Bigard.

Ellington and his band, 1941.

Duke Ellington

(b. Edward Kennedy Ellington, Washington DC, April 29 1899; d. New York City, May 24 1974)

He made his professional debut at 17 and a decade later established himself at Harlem's Cotton Club. In his five years there he became recognized as one of the world's leading jazz musicians. By 1930, with *Mood Indigo*, he was known around the world, and that renown would continue until his death (he toured the globe, and in 1971 he and his band visited the Soviet Union). With his big-band style he gave jazz a new sound, richer and more elegant. He was a relentless experimenter, and in his larger scale compositions he pushed jazz to its boundaries. He wrote film scores. He recorded widely. As André Hodeir and Gunther Schuller have written, he was "one of the first musicians to concern himself with composition and musical form in jazz— as distinct from improvisation, tune writing, and arranging."

DUKE ELLINGTON: "*I try to catch the character and mood and feeling of my people. The music of my race is something more than the American idiom. It is the result of our transplantation to American soil and was our reaction, in plantation days, to the life we lived. What we could not say openly we expressed in music. The characteristic, melancholic music of my race has been forged from the very white heat of our sorrows and our gropings. I think the music of my race is something that is going to live, something that posterity will honor in a higher sense than merely that of the music of the ballroom.*"

Ellington was alone among big band leaders in that he crafted much of his work with the distinctive styles and timbres of his long-term bandsmen in mind. His unmatched charisma and managerial aplomb lay behind this unique ability to keep a band of prima donnas together for decades on end. When his star tenor saxophonist Ben Webster growled, "Governor! You've got to pay me more money! You're workin' me to *death*," Duke replied gently, "But Ben—I can't *afford* to pay you what you're worth—*nobody* can." Ellington unfailingly came up with the right word at the right time. "If he had been born white," wrote one commentator, "he probably would have been appointed Ambassador to the Court of Saint James."

Ellington's princely demeanor, impeccable manners and dress, and serious dedication to his art made him a role model in the African-American community. In the '30s, to spare his men the humiliations of Jim-Crow hotels, restaurants, and racist police that plagued other black bands, Ellington toured nationwide in two Pullman cars where the band slept and dined.

In 1930 Ellington made a breakthrough with *Mood Indigo*, the first of dozens of song hits that were to become standards, hits such as *(In My) Solitude, In a Sentimental Mood*, and *Sophisticated Lady*. Straining against the time limit of three minutes imposed by the industry standard of the ten-inch 78-RPM record, he recorded the first extended jazz work, *Creole Rhapsody*, in 1931. He pioneered chamber jazz by featuring the "band within a band," a convention later adopted by the Benny Goodman Trio and Quartet, Bob Crosby's Bobcats, Tommy Dorsey's Clambake Seven, Chick Webb and his Little Chicks, and Count Basie's Kansas City Seven.

When his aggressive manager, Irving Mills, arranged the band's first British and European tour in 1933, Ellington was stunned to find himself lionized by classical music critics, composers, and fanatical record collectors who did not dance to his music but rather listened, convincing him his music had durability and worth, urging him toward the creation of more ambitious works like *Black, Brown and Beige: A Tone Parallel to the History of the American Negro*, which was premiered in Carnegie Hall.

When the Band seemed to have reached its peak in the late '30s, three additions thrust it to still greater heights. In 1938, Billy Strayhorn joined as staff arranger-composer-pianist and the Ellington alter ego. From the time he joined Ellington until Strayhorn's death thirty years later, few scores in which he did not have a hand found their way into the Ellington book. The band's new theme, *Take the "A" Train*, was entirely Strayhorn's doing. Few songwriters matched the lyric Ravel-inspired beauty of *Day Dream* or *Passion Flower*. If Strayhorn's ballads are not as well known as Ellington's, it may be because they are devilishly difficult to sing.

The bursting-at-the-seams tenor sax of Ben Webster, veteran of countless round-the-clock Kansas City cutting contests and master of romantic ballads, blues at any tempo, and uptempo flagwavers such as *I Got Rhythm*, joined the longtime reed quartet in 1939 to fire up a band lusting for a new voice. Since no "book" (written scores) at first existed for Ben, he had to "find his own note," imparting an indefinable wail to the reeds that sent critics back to the thesaurus for new adjectives of celebration.

The most radical innovation of all was Jimmy Blanton, the first "modern" bassist to use the instrument melodically as well as rhythmically, imparting a new drive to the band and upsetting all previous notions of bass playing, thus contriving a carryover from note to note that freed up the rhythm section. Before Blanton died of tuberculosis at 22, he convinced all future bassists from Charles Mingus, Ray Brown, and beyond that there could be no other approach to the instrument.

The triumvirate of Strayhorn, Webster, and Blanton ushered in the golden age of Ellington, documented on the important series of Victor records made from 1940 to 1945. It is important to stress that Ellington did not employ instruments unusual to jazz (such as flute,

Composer as performer.

oboe, bassoon, or French horn), but achieved his unique effects with the complement used by all other popular dance bands, such as those of Goodman and the Dorseys: three trumpets, three trombones, five saxes doubling on clarinet, and a rhythm section of piano, string bass, rhythm guitar, and drums. Ellington's piano, both as a solo and orchestral voice, had undergone swift development to become perhaps the essential voice in the ensemble. When the band played dance halls, the first few numbers might be kicked off by concertmaster Harry Carney before the Maestro made his dramatic entrance. When he sat at the piano and hit a few chords, that band was *on*. Without the piano, it was not the same.

The World War II draft cost Ellington some of his key soloists, and in this era, which devastated many of the big bands, he leaned on Strayhorn when the going got rough. Wholesale changes in the early '50s, with the arrival of trumpeter Clark Terry and drummer Louis Bellson, injected a welcome note of "modern" jazz, toward which Ellington and especially Strayhorn had been moving all along. His prolific recording schedule was divided among ambitious reworkings of older classics such as *Prelude to a Kiss* and *All Too Soon*, concert performances of *Sophisticated Lady* and *Mood Indigo*, and a flurry of extended compositions: *The Tattooed Bride*, *The Far East Suite*, the *Liberian Suite*, and *Such Sweet Thunder*, based on themes from Shakespeare.

A historic controversy in 1965 surrounded the refusal of the Pulitzer Committee to award Ellington the prize for which he had been nominated, promoting the angry resignation of some committee members. With his customary tongue-in-cheek suavity, the 66-year-old Ellington quipped, "Fate is being kind to me. Fate does not want me to become too famous, too young."

A deeply religious man who read the Bible from cover to cover several times, Ellington poured his final energies into a series of *Sacred Concerts* performed in major places of worship, including San Francisco's Grace Cathedral, and he worked steadily as composer and bandleader to the end. The passing of most jazz artists is noted in items confined to the back obituary pages. When Ellington died in 1974, at age 71, he was mourned in headlines around the world. Today, musicians of all ages and nations are still exploring the potential of his music.

The ascent of Edward Kennedy Ellington and his assured place in the pantheon of American music was foretold with uncanny clairvoyance in 1913 by the London *Times*: "We look to the future for the American composer, not, indeed, to the Horatio Parkers and Edward MacDowells of the present, who are taking over a foreign act ready-made and are imitating it,... but to someone as yet unknown...who will sing the songs of his own nation, his own time and his own character."

The *Times* of London might also have been encouraged by another composer then in his teens. Aaron Copland led a miraculously productive, multi-faceted musical life—and a long one. He composed for Carnegie Hall and Hollywood, conducted, played the piano, taught, did television shows, encouraged the young, symbolized the possibility of being a serious composer in this country in the 20th century. He never wrote inattentively nor without huge signs declaring "made in America." He was also the author of two books of blessedly demystifying clarity, *What to Listen For in Music* and *The New Music*. With his powerfully sculpted head, exuberant stride, and that smile composed in equal parts of benevolence and mischief, he was a vibrant presence.

In 1925, long before such beloved works as *Appalachian Spring* and *Lincoln Portrait* enshrined Aaron Copland as America's patriotic composer, the young Copland caught a different feeling that was as much in tune with its time as those later pieces were with theirs. "There was a

Aaron Copland

(b. Brooklyn, New York, November 14 1900; d. North Tarrytown, New York, December 2 1990)

After studies in Paris with Nadia Boulanger, he returned to this country as a young musical firebrand. During the Depression and Second World War, he became increasingly aware of what he considered the artist's responsibility to reach the broadest audience without diminishing the quality of the music. His new populist style was exemplified by his music for the ballets *Billy the Kid* (1938), *Rodeo* (1942), and *Appalachian Spring* (1944). Copland also wrote a craggier music, of which we hear examples in the Piano Variations (1930) and *Inscape* (1967). A great educator as well as a pluralist, he authored the books *What to Listen for in Music* (1939), *Our New Music* (1941, revised in 1968 as *The New Music*), and *Music and Imagination* (1952).

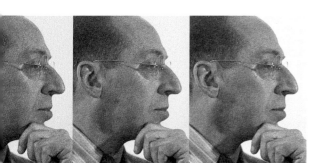

AARON COPLAND, ON HIS 1925 *MUSIC FOR THE THEATRE:* "*I was anxious to write a work that would immediately be recognized as American in character. This desire to be 'American' was symptomatic of the period.*"

lot of fun in bucking the tide," he wrote much later in his autobiography, "and feeling a part of the avant garde out there fighting new battles. That feeling was very much a part of the excitement of the times." On January 11, 1925, Walter Damrosch, having just led the premiere of Copland's Symphony for Organ and Orchestra, turned to his Carnegie Hall audience. "If a young man at the age of twenty-three can write a symphony like that," he said, "in five years he will be ready to commit murder."

One way in which Copland did not buck the tide was in going to Europe in 1921 to study composition: "In those days it was clear that you had to be 'finished' in Europe," he wrote later. "You couldn't be 'finished' in America." Planning to stay in France for one year, he had the great good fortune to become one of Nadia Boulanger's early students, and one year stretched to three.

In France, Copland began looking at his homeland with a sense of perspective. In Europe, he sensed less of a distinction between "high culture" and real life, and it was there that the seeds of his fascination with the rich diversity of his own country's music were planted. Thus began his interest in American popular music and his search for inspiration in jazz, blues, cowboy songs, and hymns. As he recalled: "The conviction grew inside me that the two things that seemed always to have been separate in America—music and the life about me—must be made to touch. This desire to make the music I wanted to write come out of the life I had lived in America became a preoccupation of mine in the twenties." The 1925 *Music for the Theatre* captures both the sounds and the spirit of vernacular theater.

From the beginning, *Appalachian Spring* has been depicted as a celebration of American folk life, as in this advertisement for a recording conducted by Copland champion Serge Koussevitzky.

In Copland's 1930 Piano Variations the vernacular spirit was submerged in a more severe style—one that Walter Damrosch might well have regarded as a reasonable fulfillment of his prophecy. This is a terse, uncompromising work (the critic B.H. Haggin always used "granitic" to characterize this kind of Copland), and it was not easily established in the repertory. Predictably, the Variations were clobbered in the New York papers. Copland himself gave the first performance of his Piano Variations in a League of Composers concert on January 4, 1931. An unsigned review in the *New York Times* regretted that Copland, "who started out in orthodox fashion not many years ago, has been attracted more and more to the 'stream of consciousness' school." Jerome D. Bohm wrote in the *Herald Tribune*: "Mr. Copland, always a composer of radical tendencies, has in these variations sardonically thumbed his nose at all those esthetic attributes which have hitherto been considered essential to the creation of music." He went on to say, sportingly, that he hoped "some day to find enjoyment in such music as Mr. Copland's." Those were prophetic words. After a 1958 performance of the orchestral version of the piece, Howard Taubman wrote in the *Times*, "The music has not changed; our capacity to respond has."

Not long after he introduced the Piano Variations, Copland began consciously to try communicating to a larger segment of the public. "I felt that it was worth the effort to see if I couldn't say what I had to say in the simplest possible terms." It was a turnaround that both reflected and affected Depression-era America. "What is the process," Michael Tilson Thomas has pondered, "wherein somebody who is a young, wild-eyed radical maverick composer gradually becomes a symbol of every conceivable solid American family value and ultimately the patriarch—the musical father—of the nation? A lot of this process had to do with social and political trends of the day. In the '30s, radical musical circles—and Aaron was a part of those—were tremendously interested in folklore as a source for a recognizable musical language for all Americans, a language that could come out of the past. The music could invent the kind of past that perhaps never existed—a kind of music in which people could find themselves. Particularly with the coming of the war, this was Aaron's real direction: to make the notes be a reflection of various kinds of folklore—Appalachian tunes, cowboy tunes, Latin-American music, blue notes from Jewish music, blue notes from African-American music. All these elements have as their central message a kind of generosity and inclusiveness. This was not an easy step for him to take; he was much attacked and questioned by members of the avant-garde school. But his motivation—to give the nation a strength of mutual respect and recognition, which it could find in music perhaps more immediately than in daily life—was something in which he believed totally."

The 1947 *In the Beginning*, composed in response to a commission from Harvard University, continued Copland's tribute to America—in this

Aaron Copland and Michael Tilson Thomas in the 1980s.

Aaron Copland, maverick-turned-patriarch.

case, he took inspiration from the tradition of Yankee singing schools. Yet the exacting score, a setting (in English) of the first chapter of Genesis and the first few verses of the second chapter, reflects a jazz-tinged modernism: "It does not incorporate folk music or jazz materials," Copland wrote, "but jazz rhythms are used in various sections, particularly for the verse 'And let there be light in the firmament of the heavens....'" Soprano Bridgett Hooks, soloist in this work in the American Mavericks festival, notes that "Copland's use of complex rhythmic patterns [i.e., duples counter to triples] brings the text alive and depicts the creation in an explosive way." She feels that, though often described as "jazzy," the work's "rhythmic vitality and declamatory text" also evoke the tradition of the African-American spiritual. Henry Dreger, Jr., a member of the San Francisco Symphony Chorus, notes the way Copland's dissonances (half steps between chorus and soloists, and between men and women in the chorus) evoke the "restlessness of creation." "The final 'soul' is a plain E-flat major chord. The restlessness has stopped and we have arrived 'home.'"

If Copland took to original source material as a point of departure for his works of Americana (and also for several works of Latin Americana), he also took pleasure in the sources themselves. In 1950, he arranged a group of five *Old American Songs* for voice and small orchestra. His settings of these tunes proved so popular that, two years later, he arranged five more songs from our country's past. Copland, it seemed, had established himself against all argument as one of those artists—a Whitman, a Steinbeck, a Remington, a Dorothea Lange—who expressed the essence of America.

But it was also in the 1950s that some composers, including a few for whom no one would have thought it likely, discovered the possibilities of serial composition, Arnold Schoenberg's innovations and their ramifications. Stravinsky was the greatest eminence among these, but Copland definitely belongs on the list. He wrote just four such compositions—the Piano Quartet (1950), the Piano Fantasy (1957), *Connotations* (1962), and *Inscape* (1967)—but they are a strong group indeed.

Serialism is a compositional technique. It is *not* a style, a manner, a tone of voice. To put it with perhaps dangerous brevity, what is involved in serial writing is the composer's decision to relate his choices of pitches to a particular ordering of the twelve notes, the ordering being chosen specifically for the work in question. (Composer John Adams has aptly referred to this ordering as the genetic code of the piece.) In the '20s and '30s, however, that technique was so powerfully associated with the work of Arnold Schoenberg that Copland was not alone in finding that it had not occurred to him "to try to separate the method from the aesthetic." The aesthetic made him uncomfortable. The technique or the method, on the other hand, Copland found interesting. "I was interested in the simple outlines of the theory and in adapting them to my own purposes," he told Phillip Ramey in the liner notes for the Columbia recording of *Connotations.* "As a result I began to hear chords I wouldn't have heard otherwise; here was a new way of moving tones about that had a freshening effect on one's technique and approach."

Copland's willingness to seek out techniques to refresh his style illustrates that he was more than a wonderful composer, and he was also a more versatile one than we sometimes make him out to be. It is a critical cliché that there are two Coplands, one being the composer of popular essays in Americana—both urban, such as *Music for the Theatre* and *El Salón México,* and pastoral, such as *Billy the Kid* and *Appalachian Spring*—and the other the composer of more severe, certainly more abstract, less referential works such as the Piano Variations and his late orchestral score *Inscape.* The two Coplands are one, and the two styles are connected, each drawing strength and substance from the other. He was also a complete citizen of the music world. Well after he had become our most celebrated composer, even as he was getting on in years, one could still see him at new-music concerts in the most unglamorous locales, keeping track, ready with an encouraging word to his young colleagues—"keeping the faith," as Milton Babbitt remarked on one of those occasions.

"It was a Copland talent," Vivian Perlis has written, "to face each occasion with anticipation, fresh spirit, and genuine pleasure." He recalled having asked himself early in his career why, if there was a French-sounding music and a German sound, there could not be an American sound as well. "We had done it in ragtime and jazz, but not in the kind of concert music I was interested in." Looking at Copland's career, we can trace his pursuit of the answer to that question, from the craggy works of his young years to those that established him as our "musical patriarch."

Virgil Thomson once said that American music was any music written by an American. Perhaps. But Duke Ellington and Aaron Copland had other ideas. Each looked to the music of the people and created a music for the people—reminding all who hear it of a uniquely American sound, inseparable from the cultural fabric of this country. Their best-known efforts are elegant and engaging—certainly less aggressively radical than those of the modernists. Yet their perpetual willingness to cross musical and cultural boundaries—and to challenge even such stereotypes as they had helped create—offer a compelling argument for a less doctrinaire definition of *maverick.*

chapter five

EW SOURCES OF MUSICAL SOUND: Technology and the Junkyard

GEORGE ANTHEIL

CONLON NANCARROW

LOU HARRISON

JOHN CAGE (I)

The effect of technology on everyday life was arguably the most dramatic feature of the 20th century. Yet even as audiences struggled to assimilate the revolutionary impact of radio, telephone, phonograph, and the automobile, most composers clung to traditional ensembles as vehicles for musical expression. Trying to capture the spirit of the new "machine age" using instrumental technology that had evolved alongside powdered wigs and horse-drawn carriages, however, proved frustrating for visionaries on both sides of the Atlantic. In Europe, the futurists, led by Luigi Russolo (1885-1947), advocated abandoning conventional instruments in favor of "noise-sound." In the United States, Edgard Varèse led the call for the "liberation of sound" by new instruments that were unhindered by human capacity. Surprising as it may seem today, one of these cutting-edge instruments, now consigned to the nostalgic past, was the player piano. Two of its champions—Americans George Antheil and Conlon Nancarrow—are only now re-emerging from the obscurity where they had dwelt as historical curiosities.

Although new inventions may have provided the initial creative stimulus, the liberation of sound was more than a result of new technology. Henry Cowell's radical methods of extracting sound from the piano, discussed in Chapter Three, opened his students and colleagues to the possibilities of using conventional instruments in unconventional ways and to adapting Instruments from other musical cultures; from there, it was a short step to expanding the sound-palette with objects not formerly considered musical instruments. Lou Harrison and John Cage were fellow Californians who haunted area junkyards in search of interesting sounds. The quantity and variety of new timbres thus created is one of the most distinguishing features of 20th-century music.

CONTRIBUTORS TO THIS CHAPTER:
PAUL D. LEHRMAN (ANTHEIL), JOHN
ADAMS (NANCARROW), MICHAEL
STEINBERG (HARRISON AND CAGE),
AND JAMES M. KELLER (CAGE)

George Antheil's *Ballet mécanique* was a work that could only have been conceived in one place and time: the hotbed of revolutionary art and letters that was Paris in the 1920s. Living among the most celebrated avant-garde artists—among them Igor Stravinsky, James Joyce, Ernest Hemingway, Gertrude Stein, Ezra Pound, Jean Cocteau, Marcel Duchamp, and Pablo Picasso—Antheil was inspired to write what could still be considered the most outrageous piece of concert music ever composed.

In 1922, Antheil toured Europe as a concert pianist and caused a sensation with his recitals of standard repertory and his own ultramodern compositions for piano, such as the *Sonata Sauvage*, *Mechanisms*, and *Airplane Sonata*, which celebrated a Jazz Age industrial aesthetic. Antheil's first year in Europe was spent mostly in Berlin, but at the end of 1923, wanting to be near the man he considered his greatest hero, Stravinsky, he moved to Paris. He took up residence in the Latin Quarter at the epicenter of Parisian belles-lettres, in a one-room apartment above Shakespeare & Company, the legendary English-language bookstore. Sylvia Beach, the store's owner, was the first publisher of Joyce's *Ulysses* and the plaintiff in the book's obscenity trial in the United States. She introduced Antheil to her circle, and the brash young American who respected no boundaries was immediately accepted into the heady scene. Soon, with violinist Olga Rudge, he introduced music he had written for her at the request of her lover, Ezra Pound, the Second Sonata for Violin with Accompaniment of Piano and Drums. This chamber work was soon followed by larger productions that revealed a composer determined to leave his mark: in 1924 the *Ballet mécanique*, and in 1925 the *Jazz Symphony*.

George Antheil in his Paris days.

Enamored with the industrial age and what he called the "anti-expressive, anti-romantic, coldly mechanistic aesthetic of the early twenties," not to mention the dadaist, surrealist, and anarchist movements that swirled around him, Antheil wrote music that celebrated machines as music-makers. He achieved great notoriety for his efforts. At the Paris premiere of *Mechanisms*, Erik Satie leaned out of his box and cried, "*Quel précision!*" It didn't hurt that Antheil was a shameless self-promoter, planting stories in the newspapers about being eaten by lions in Africa, and living up to a *soi-disant* image as an American "gangster": In Budapest, he got the audience's attention by pulling out a revolver and placing it on the piano.

The *Ballet mécanique* was Antheil's most ambitious expression of this industrial theme. Originally, it was to be a soundtrack for an abstract film of the same name by the artist Fernand Léger, photographer Man Ray, and American cinematographer Dudley Murphy. The film was

Reconstructing Antheil's *Ballet mécanique* with Computer Technology

The original, sixteen-pianola *Ballet mécanique* remained unplayed for seventy-five years. In the spring of 1999, the Ensemble Modern performed the piece in Europe and England using two player-grand pianos, custom-modified by Dr. Jürgen Hocker to be controlled by a computer. A much larger effort to produce a published version, to be played on sixteen player pianos, and performable by any group with the appropriate resources, resulted in the first performance of the piece using its full orchestration, at a public college in Massachusetts in November 1999.

The original manuscript of the 1924 *Ballet mécanique* was in a large collection of Antheil's papers placed in the care of San Francisco Bay Area composer Charles Amirkhanian by Antheil's widow, Böske, in 1978. Over the next several years, Amirkhanian, also a musicologist and the executive director of San Francisco's Other Minds, made copies of the scores available to performers under the imprint "Antheil Press." In 1992, the original manuscripts were sold to the Performing Arts Division of the New York Public Library, and the publishing rights were assigned to G. Schirmer.

William Holab, then Publications Director at Schirmer and an expert on computer applications in music, saw an opportunity to use modern MIDI technology to accomplish what Antheil and Pleyel could not. MIDI (Musical Instrument Digital Interface) is the standard digital protocol for communications between electronic musical devices and is used by countless composers, performers, arrangers, and publishers. Modern player pianos, which are available from a number of manufacturers, no longer use the paper-roll-controlled pneumatically driven mechanisms of their ancestors, but instead use small MIDI-speaking computers to drive banks of solenoids that move the keys, hammers, and dampers. Hooked up to a MIDI network, any number of such player pianos could be controlled and synchronized tightly.

Holab contacted Michael Bates, head of academic relations at Yamaha, whose extensive line of MIDI-compatible player pianos are called Disklaviers, to see if the manufacturer would support one or more initial performances of the revived *Ballet*. Bates agreed enthusiastically. In 1998, after freelance editor George McGuire had painstakingly prepared a computer-engraved score from Antheil's original manuscript, Holab contacted me to see if I would be interested in doing the necessary programming to convert the written pianola parts into a MIDI "sequence" file that could be played by a computer. Although I knew of the 1952 version of the piece, having been introduced to it in high school by a percussion teacher, news of this older version was a complete surprise to me. I told Holab I would be delighted.

The process of converting Antheil's parts—1240 measures long, containing up to a thousand notes per measure, and incorporating some 630 time-signature changes—into a MIDI sequence took several months. The process was not simply one of transcription. To ensure that my work was as historically accurate as possible, I consulted various literary sources such as Antheil's autobiography, other books and essays from the era, and collections of clippings and letters at Columbia University and the New York Public Library, as well as a number of player piano experts. At the Library, I discovered a "pre-original" manuscript for four pianolas alone, which Antheil apparently had given to Pleyel to cut the first piano rolls. Many hours were spent examining and resolving inconsistencies between the manuscripts in an effort to make the final product as close to the composer's intentions as possible.

As I was working with the piano parts, I recognized that performing groups might not have easy access to sirens, bells, and airplane propellers, and so I collected digital recordings of those sounds and saved them as computer files. These sounds, in various formats for different "samplers," are now part of the rental materials that Schirmer issues to groups wishing to play the piece. The airplanes were recorded by Tim Tully at a private airfield in San Carlos, California; the siren was recorded at the central fire house in Arlington, Massachusetts; and the bells, obtained from a variety of hardware stores and Internet sources, were record-

The original *Ballet mécanique*, reconstructed, was given its West Coast premiere by the San Francisco Symphony and 16 Yamaha Disklaviers, conducted by Michael Tilson Thomas.

ed in my own studio in Medford, Massachusetts. In addition, my university colleague Coleman Rogers and I built a device that would allow the bell sounds to be played "live": Seven different-sized electric bells are turned on and off with MIDI commands generated by a computer (the same one that is controlling the player pianos), or by a human performer using a standard MIDI keyboard.

Another issue that had to be dealt with was who was going to follow whom, the pianolas or the conductor. Although the piece has a huge number of time-signature changes, the tempo does not change at all. So should the conductor be free to push and pull the tempo as he sees fit? Or should the conductor be a slave to the machines? MIDI sequencing programs are able to track tempo changes from human sources such as levers or "tap" pads fairly well, but most of them are designed to work with simple, steady time signatures—not the 11/16, 7/32, 40/8, and other outrageous meters that Antheil wrote—so it seemed much more practical to have the conductor follow the computer, and thus keep the human players in sync with the player pianos, than to try to do it the other way around. Therefore, I created a complicated "click track," along with some recorded voice cues indicating rehearsal letters, for the conductor to follow, and he listens to it through a headphone.

Yet another issue was tempo. The only tempo marking in Antheil's scores was the cryptic "Pianola=85." According to English pianola expert Rex Lawson, this does not mean eighty-five beats per minute; it means that the piano rolls were to be fed through the mechanism at 8.5 feet per minute. Lawson owns copies of the original Pleyel rolls, and measuring the distance between the notes on those rolls, he calculated that the desired tempo was 152 beats per minute. This correlates well with the 1952 version of the piece, in which the tempo is marked "Allegro (feroce) quarter-note =144:160."

Unfortunately, the 1924 version is completely unplayable at anything approaching this tempo. The xylophone and human-piano parts are too fast, and the bass drum parts are too rhythmically complex, for live performers to play the piece at a tempo greater than about 120. Even the Yamaha Disklaviers, which can reproduce the fastest human piano technique imaginable, start losing notes at about 133 beats per minute, and that only after much tweaking of the parts to maximize the instruments' ability to play at high speed. So far, performances of this new version of the piece have been played at 90, 100, and 115 beats per minute—the last conducted by Michael Tilson Thomas.

The Schirmer project came to a culmination in the fall of 1999, when I produced a concert at the University of Massachusetts Lowell, featuring conductor Jeffrey Fischer and the school's percussion ensemble playing the world premiere of the new version, before an audience of a thousand. Yamaha supplied sixteen Disklaviers through a local dealer. The concert was simultaneously webcast through the facilities of the local public radio station, WGBH. The piece was subsequently recorded, and a CD of that recording—which also includes works by John Cage and Lou Harrison, Amadeo Roldàn, Richard Grayson, and Felix Mendelssohn (in an arrangement for multiple player pianos by this writer), all of which were also on the concert—is now available on the Electronic Music Foundation label. On April 2, 2000, the *Ballet mécanique* received its New York premiere at Carnegie Hall, performed by the American Composers Orchestra under the baton of Dennis Russell Davies, with Disklaviers (eight of them) again supplied by Yamaha. ▶   – P A U L   D .   L E H R M A N

completed (and can be found today in various "history of avant-garde cinema" compilations), but almost immediately the two works diverged—for one thing, the music ended up being twice as long as the film. They were premiered separately and have since been presented together only rarely.

But the music itself was a problem: 1240 measures of brutal rhythms, noise, snatches of melody, and silence, provided by sixteen player pianos playing four different parts, two grand pianos, seven electric bells, three xylophones, four bass drums, a tam-tam, a siren, and three airplane propellers. The piece requires a great deal of precision and synchronization among the player pianos. Synchronized player pianos (or "pianolas," as they were often called) existed only in theory, however. Pleyel, a Paris piano manufacturer with whom Antheil worked closely, designed and even took out a patent on a system of synchronizing mechanisms that could be used with a number of different entertainment-oriented devices, including player pianos, which bear no small resemblance in principal to the systems that today synchronize video and audio electronically. But it seems that Pleyel was never able to build a working model of the system—with the result that Antheil had nothing to play his piece on. In private concerts in 1925, he performed the *Ballet mécanique* on a single pianola, but obviously this could only have provided an intimation of his expansive artistic vision.

After several months of making excuses for the delay (one tale he spread was that there was no hall, in all of Paris, with sufficient electrical capability to power sixteen pianolas), Antheil re-wrote the *Ballet mécanique* for a single pianola and made up for the loss by expanding the parts to be played by a phalanx of human pianists. Even without the sixteen pianolas, the piece was a sensation. Several private performances at various salons in Paris, in which the audiences

George Antheil and friends, Paris, 1925.

George Antheil

(b. Trenton, New Jersey, July 8 1900; d. New York City, February 12 1959)

He called himself the **Bad Boy of Music**, and in his early works he set a premium on shock value, with scores that include parts for airplane propellers and player pianos. Antheil's father was a shoe salesman; his German-born mother was a housewife. George showed great promise as a musician at an early age and began composing at 11. He made headlines with his radical works, including the *Ballet mécanique*. He penned a column for *Esquire*, dispensed advice to the lovelorn, and authored four books—a murder mystery, a treatise on criminology, a volume predicting military strategy in the Second World War, and his autobiography. He teamed with actress Hedy Lamarr in designing a jam-proof radio guidance system for torpedoes. In his later years his audience dwindled and his music became more conservative. He moved to Vienna, then Berlin, and eventually the United States. He scored a number of Hollywood films, including Stanley Kramer's 1957 epic *The Pride and the Passion*.

were well-lubricated with champagne, were the talk of the town. Its public premiere at the Théâtre Champs Élysées on June 19, 1926 was proclaimed by Sylvia Beach as "one of the most significant artistic events of the 1920s."

Bravig Imbs, an American writer, described the scene: "People began to call each other names and to forget that there was any music going on at all. Ezra Pound took advantage [of a lull] to jump to his feet and yell, *'Vous êtes tous des imbéciles!'* [You are all imbeciles!] One fat, bald old gentleman who had been particularly disagreeable lashed out his umbrella, opened it, and pretended to be struggling against the imaginary gale of wind from the electric fans [substituting for propellers]. His gesture was immediately copied by many.... When the *Ballet* was over, George got an ovation that was greater than the catcalls, for everyone was willing to applaud a man who had at least accomplished something."

After the concert, out in the streets, fistfights broke out between the composer's supporters and his detractors. It was the greatest riot at any musical event since the premiere more than a decade earlier of Stravinsky's *Le Sacre du printemps*—in fact, Aaron Copland wrote that Antheil had succeeded in "out-sacking the *Sacre*." Said Antheil: "From this moment on I knew that, for a time at least, I would be the new darling of Paris. Paris loves you for giving it a good fight, and an artistic scandal does not raise aristocratic lorgnettes."

Antheil's reputation followed him around Europe, and all of his subsequent concerts were Events of the highest order. In 1927, a New York promoter arranged to bring the *Ballet* to Carnegie Hall, hyping it to the hilt, repeating and exaggerating the story of the Paris premiere, and not-at-all-subtly hinting that there might well be a public uproar at Carnegie as well.

But it was a dismal failure. Provocateurs hired to create disturbances at the back of the hall were ignored. Two huge murals—one of a cityscape and another of a dancing African-American couple (to evoke the spirit of Antheil's *Jazz Symphony*, also premiering that evening)—provoked laughter. This time, the propellers/fans were pointed right at the audience, and when they cranked up, people had to clutch their programs and hats with both hands to keep them from blowing away. One audience member reportedly attached a white handkerchief to the end of his cane and waved it at

A prophet of machinery and music from Trenton, N. J., and Paris, France, presenting his Ballet Mecanique and other discoveries at Carnegie Hall to-morrow evening.

Antheil, as seen by a cartoonist in a New York newspaper of the 1920s.

the stage in mock surrender. The siren player, who had had no chance to rehearse, didn't realize that his instrument needed to warm up before it would sound, so when the cue came from the conductor, he started cranking furiously, but no sound emerged. After the piece ended, the siren, finally up to speed, sang out a solo. Reviewers were almost unanimous in their ridicule of the concert and its composer. At least one made sneering reference to "trying to make a mountain out of an Antheil."

Antheil went back to Paris, dejected. But the honeymoon in Europe had ended as well. In the years since he first conceived the *Ballet mécanique*, his tastes had changed, and he was (like Stravinsky) writing in a more tonal, neoclassical vein. Among his works from this period was an opera, *Transatlantic*, which was a satire of American politics and which was premiered — and very well received — in Frankfurt in May 1930. But with the specter of Nazism rising, new operas, especially written by non-Germans, were becoming increasingly unwelcome at German opera houses.

Antheil, his composing career at an impasse and also facing the realization that Europe was soon to enter a devastating war, returned to the United States for good in 1933. He continued to compose concert music but made his living elsewhere. He wrote books and articles on various subjects (and even, for a brief time, a lonely hearts column syndicated by *Esquire* magazine) and finally settled in Hollywood, where he established a successful, if somewhat unsung, niche writing scores for films and working with such movie legends as Stanley Kramer, Ben Hecht, and Cecil B. De Mille.

Like Antheil, Conlon Nancarrow found the traditional world of orchestral instruments too confining and the technique of the people who played them too limiting to express his musical ideas. Inspiration came from two sources: Stravinsky's *Le Sacre du printemps,* which he had heard as a college student, and which convinced him that composing was his calling, and Henry Cowell's *New Musical Resources* (published in 1930), which set him on the path he would follow. In his book, Cowell discussed the possibility of subdividing a rhythmic unit — i.e., a whole note — into different fractions — i.e., thirds, fourths, and fifths — and playing them simultaneously. "Some of the rhythms developed through the present acoustical investigation could not be played by any living performer," he admitted, then suggested that "these highly engrossing rhythmical complexes could easily be cut on a player-piano roll. This would give a real reason for writing music specifically for player-piano, such as music written for it at present does not seem to have."

Nancarrow became absorbed — one could easily say he was obsessed — with Cowell's idea of what might happen if two or more melodic lines, each traveling at a different speed, were to be played at the same time. The desire for the "polytemporal" (as opposed to the merely polyrhythmic) drove Nancarrow to the recourse of composing most of his music directly for the piano roll. By painstakingly punching in every note and every duration onto the paper roll, Nancarrow was able to achieve a level of exactitude that would be more or less impossible to realize in the messy human world of live performers. In the decades before personal computers, Nancarrow virtually abandoned composing for live performers and took his rhythmic explorations to the *ne plus ultra*. In one study after another for player piano, he forged ahead into the uncharted terrain of rhythmic complexity with the undaunted zeal of a New World explorer.

Living and working in controversial political exile in Mexico, Nancarrow did not begin to achieve notoriety until the 1970s, when Charles Amirkhanian of Berkeley began a project of recording his complete "Studies" for player piano for 1750 Arch Records. Between 1977 and 1985, the composer Peter Garland published a large number of the "scores" for these studies in his magazine, *Soundings*. Within the next decade Nancarrow's discoveries began to exert a profound influence on contemporary composers in both Europe and the United States. Composers as different in taste and technique as György Ligeti, Elliott Carter, and Harrison Birtwistle showed strong traces of their exposure to Nancarrow in their music.

The strength of Nancarrow lies not only in his bold, ofttimes outrageous use of rhythm and simultaneity of tempi, but also in his whimsical taste for the vernacular. Especially in the earlier studies, he draws his actual musical "material" from very familiar sources: ragtime, blues,

Conlon Nancarrow in his Mexico City Studio: Lights, pencils, piano rolls.

Conlon Nancarrow

(b. Texarkana, Arkansas, October 27 1912; d. Mexico City, August 10 1997)

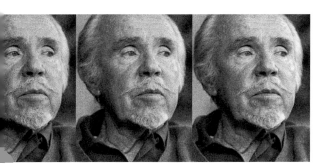

He started out as a trumpet player, both jazz and classical, and he went on to study with Nicolas Slonimsky, Walter Piston, and Roger Sessions. A maverick in more than music, he returned to the United States from the Spanish Civil War only to run into trouble with the government because of his socialist views. After a brief stint in New York, where he contributed a radio column to the journal *Modern Music*, he moved to Mexico City in 1940 and lived there the rest of his life. Frustrated because performers could not manage the difficult rhythms of his music, he began composing for player piano, punching his own piano rolls and creating showpieces of virtuosity that are faster and more brilliant, and with chords more widely spaced, than any human being could hope to play. Only in the 1970s did recordings introduce his work to more than a few.

boogie-woogie, habanera, flamenco, even big-band swing. One might even venture to surmise that, had Nancarrow couched his remarkable discoveries in the more severe language of serialism, his music may not have had the powerful effect on the music world that it did. As Nancarrow biographer Kyle Gann writes, "The measure of his achievement is that music so complicated in description sounds so vivid and direct. The music invites participation by the brain because it first made such intuitive sense to the ear."

In the early 1990s, the American pianist Yvar Mikhashoff (1941-93) approached Nancarrow about making orchestrations of some of these studies. Mikhashoff rightly reasoned that Nancarrow had, years before, resorted to the piano roll only out of desperation, feeling that no human performer could ever realize the extreme precision his music required. By the 1990s, however, skills among performers had evolved so dramatically that performing complex polytemporal pieces was less an impossibility than it had been when Nancarrow had begun to compose. With the composer's blessing (or, more likely, his grumbling assent—he was a maverick, after all), Mikhashoff orchestrated nearly a dozen of the studies and recorded them with the Ensemble Modern. The result was a revelation, largely because the color and personality of instruments played by living, breathing performers brought out formerly unnoticed details and delights in the music and allowed a new generation of listeners to appreciate one of America's most idiosyncratic musical voices.

Lou Harrison in 1949.

Lou Harrison spent his childhood in the rich cultural environment of San Francisco, where his family moved when he was 9. In San Francisco, Harrison studied Gregorian chant at Mission Dolores, went to dance class (where he and his brother dutifully learned to maneuver their way through waltzes, schottisches, and polkas), and listened with curiosity and delight to whatever music came out of the Chinese and Japanese communities. It was a varied diet that led naturally to a life in which, along with being a prolific composer, Harrison has at different times been a florist, record clerk, poet, music and dance critic, music copyist, and playwright. Versatility and flexibility have always been among his outstanding attributes, and there seem to be no barriers of geography and history that stand between him and the world's music.

A Visit With Lou Harrison

Lou Harrison is a figure so lively and forward-looking that the word "senior" sits oddly upon him—although at 84 he can be said to have earned it. He is a West Coast phenomenon. To visit him at his house in Aptos is first of all to be reminded of why people love to live in California. The house is on what he calls the third story above sea level, with just the sort of spectacular view of the Pacific that this suggests, but Lou immediately adds that the way the world is going it may well be the second story before long.

Before we settle in the lush garden to talk, I get a quick tour of the house, where the beautiful, the practical, and the enchantingly kitschy cohabit harmoniously and happily. Just to the left of the main entrance is the subtly lit gamelan room—its official name is the Ives Room—its ample floor area covered with bronze, iron, wood, and bamboo instruments, all built by Lou's late partner, William Colvig, who died in March 2000. The room shows California at its best, an open world, and so the gamelan shares space with a clavichord, several reed organs, and a beautifully carved, brown 1871 Steinway grand piano that was the favorite West Coast instrument of the Australian composer and pianist Percy Grainger, a figure whose disinclination to believe that wonderful music happened only in Europe and was produced only by white men makes him highly simpatico to Lou.

In the garden, Lou shows me a fine growth of English roses, these being raised not only for their looks but to ensure a supply of rose hips for rose-hip tea and jam. His face, white-bearded, is open and serious, the eyes almost alarmingly scrutinous, but when he is amused and goes into his laugh mode, it happens without warning or modulation, the jaw drops like that of an old-fashioned nutcracker, and the whole structure is realigned in a smile of totally enveloping warmth.

I ask Lou about what some have seen as a division between East Coast and West Coast music, the Atlantic/Pacific thing. His immediate response is that one of the salient differences is the interest on the part of West Coast composers in new instruments and new tunings—new to traditional European-based music, that is: "None of us can resist making or incorporating new instruments." Lou's music includes ranch triangles, sleighbells, big bells made from large, gassed-out oxygen tanks that are struck with baseball bats, the deep, bossed gong of the Javanese gamelan, spoons, tack piano, iron pipes, brake drums, elephant bells, tongued teponaztli (a Mexican slit drum), tuned rice bowls, and bakers' pans. Among his allies in this kind of exploring of colors and textures, Lou mentions Henry Cowell, Janice Giteck, Morgan Powell, and of course Harry Partch, one of the boldest of all the explorers, inventor of many new instruments (among them seventy-two-string kitharas, boos, cloud-chamber bowls, and blow-boys), and the proponent of a forty-three-note scale.

Another vitally essential mentor—along with Cowell, John Cage (to whom he was also bound in close friendship), Virgil Thomson, and the Korean musician Lee Hye-Ku—has been his own Javanese gamelan teacher, Pak Chokro. Lou says of him: "There's nothing you could hope to surprise him with. Like Henry Cowell, he's all for mixing it up and having a good time." That double encomium says it all.

Lou loves it when people care about his music, and he makes no bones about that. At the same time, he notes ruefully that the beautiful house at the top of Aptos has virtually become a business office, where the telephone answering machine and the fax are constantly engaged. Invitations to concerts, schools, conferences, and symposia come in constantly, and so do requests for new compositions. Lou tells me that he has recently bought a set of CDs of the Beethoven string quartets. He shakes his head, laughs the Lou Harrison laugh, and says, "Maybe I'll actually have time to listen to one or two before I die." Busoni said that only he who looks ahead is truly happy. To see that in action, go to the hilltop in Aptos. ❯ —MICHAEL STEINBERG

In 1934, Lou Harrison became a student of Henry Cowell, which was probably the single most critical decision of his musical life, and although the formal teacher-pupil relationship went on for only one year, the deep friendship endured until Cowell's death in 1965. Harrison remembers with special gratitude a course on what later came to be called "world music" that Cowell taught for the extension division of the University of California at San Francisco.

At Cowell's suggestion, Harrison went to Los Angeles to work with Schoenberg. It is hard to imagine two composers more different than Arnold Schoenberg and Lou Harrison, but Schoenberg was not the rigid sort of musician he is often made out to be—he had, for example, invited Cowell to play for his composition class in Berlin in the 1920s—and the relationship, though brief, was thoroughly cordial. Harrison remembers Schoenberg fondly: "He was very open and he took *you* seriously." The class was set up as a kind of Platonic symposium. "Schoenberg constantly moved me, and all his students, in the direction of simplicity—bring out *only the salient*; and when he dismissed me, he urged me above all to study Mozart." Harrison notes extraordinary similarities between what he was taught about orchestration by Schoenberg and later by Virgil Thomson, another pair of composers who could hardly be more different. Among his fellow students, Harrison particularly remembers the teenage Dika Newlin, who went on to write one of the first important books in English about Schoenberg, and the photographer Harold Halma, "author of the famous picture of Truman Capote *en odalisque.*"

After Los Angeles, Cowell, as Harrison puts it, "spread me around." He got him jobs, the first of them as accompanist for Tina Flade's modern dance classes at Mills College, an association that led to his becoming expert in Labanotation for dance. In the 1940s, Lou Harrison had his East Coast period. Again through Cowell, he had met Virgil Thomson, that fascinating amalgam of Kansas City and the Champs Élysées, who had moved back to America after many years in Europe to become the *Herald Tribune*'s music critic. Not only did Thomson himself, on his best nights, spark true glory years in the history of music criticism in America, but he engaged younger writers who also added to the luster of the *Tribune*'s arts pages. Harrison was one of these. At the same time, Harrison contributed to that invaluable journal *Modern Music*, served as editor for New Music Editions, and conducted. It was he who, in 1947, led the first complete performance of a symphony by Charles Ives—No. 3, a work then thirty-eight years old. The Ives connection continued. Harrison was one of the musicians involved in preparing the often chaotic manuscripts for

American gamelan instruments built by Lou Harrison and William Colvig.

Lou Harrison

(b. Portland, Oregon, May 14 1917)

The Grand Master of San Francisco Bay Area composers, he is a longtime resident of Aptos and co-founder of the Cabrillo Festival. He has been witness to most of the major developments of 20th-century American music, and he championed Charles Ives when Ives was better known as insurance executive than composer. Like John Cage, he worked as dance accompanist and studied with Arnold Schoenberg. He served as music critic for the *New York Herald Tribune* and taught at Black Mountain College before returning to California in the mid-'50s. A mystic and visionary, he is fascinated with Asian music and incorporates the sound of the Javanese gamelan into his own works, bridging the gap between East and West.

William Colvig at American gamelan instruments.

publication and performance, and he became one of the heirs of the Ives estate, something that has allowed him to do much quiet good in the music world. The Cabrillo Festival, devoted primarily to contemporary music and commanding an audience of unsurpassed loyalty and enthusiasm, is another one of Lou Harrison's gifts to music.

Henry Cowell's influence led Harrison to pioneer the use of found objects as sound-makers; eventually his fascination with alternate tuning systems and the expressive hardware of the East led to his designing and building his own instruments. Most of these fell into the category of percussion, with the result that this section tends to dominate in Harrison's music. As San Francisco Symphony percussionist Jack Van Geem says, "The role of the percussion section changes from one primarily of adding color or a rhythmic 'spine' to a more central role; the possibilities are expanded to bring new means to the concert hall. In Lou Harrison's music, the percussion is rooted in a melodic tradition. I think of his rhythms as melody. He's the one composer I know who writes counter-rhythms as lyrical counterpoint."

As percussionist Anthony Cirone recalls, "Lou and I had a magnificent working relationship at San Jose State University for the seventeen years we taught together. Being such a prolific composer, he wrote many works for my percussion ensemble, which I would then have the privilege of premiering at my university concerts. His partner, Bill Colvig, would build most of the instruments and provide my group with on-site instructions in assembling and playing his original creations." Cirone remembers that when Harrison and Colvig built their American gamelan, they taught such techniques as "ganza," borrowed from Indonesian music, in which the performer muffles one instrument while simultaneously striking another.

Even when writing for more conventional instruments, Harrison calls on new sonorities. His Organ Concerto is a good example, combining the solo instrument with percussion, wood drums built by Colvig, and oxygen tanks. Organist John Walker, also a faculty colleague of Harrison's at San Jose State, describes the experience of playing Harrison's concerto: "I have always found a great thrill in performance of the Organ Concerto, as it presents musical and technical challenges not encountered in traditional organ repertory. Perhaps the most Eurocentric of all musical instruments, the pipe organ has little repertory that incorporates Eastern musical rhetoric. Suddenly, in one composition, Lou Harrison has given us a masterpiece in which the organ acquires an Asian accent with the rhythmic clarity of percussion instruments. This composition forces the organist to move 'outside the envelope' of tradition. In place of standard keyboard fingerings, which yield the seamless *legato* associated with organ sonority, the player must find solutions to generate maximum rhythmic clarity. Indeed, the opening and closing movements include extensive sections in which the palm of the hand replaces the fingers on the keys, as well as sections requiring wooden slabs of one- and two-octave lengths to depress all white or black keys simultaneously, a skill one does not acquire by mastering Bach, Franck, and Messiaen! Throughout the score, the organist is challenged to project the instrument with the rhythmic clarity and vitality of the percussion orchestra."

Lou Harrison's path toward a new world of sound crossed that of John Cage, though the two arrived at widely separate aesthetic destinations. Cage's original inspiration came from immigrant German filmmaker Oskar Fischinger's notion of the correlation between an object's sound and its spiritual essence. One day Fischinger's wife dropped a key in another room. He was fascinated with the fact that he could ascertain immediately the identity of the object, and he went on to postulate that an object's characteristic sound was an emanation of its spirit—for Fischinger, evidence of the unity between the outward, material world of science and the inner truth of spirituality. For Cage, this implied an expanded and idealized conception of musical sound to include objects that were not conventional musical instruments. As Cage often stated when recalling Fischinger's impact on his own music:

John Cage and colleagues in 1941, rehearsing Lou Harrison's Simfony No. 13, for percussion. Clockwise, from left: Cage, Xenia Cage, Harrison, Margaret Jansen, Doris Dennison (back to camera).

[Fischinger] made a remark to me which dropped me into the world of noise. He said: "Everything in the world has a spirit, and this spirit becomes audible by its being set into vibration." He started me on a path of exploration of the world around me which has never stopped—of hitting and scratching and scraping and rubbing everything, with anything I can get my hands on.

Welcome to the unpredictable world of John Cage. He had made stabs at a formal music education but didn't cotton much to what he encountered in the process. At UCLA he attended classes given by Arnold Schoenberg, who in the end declared, "He is not a composer, but an inventor—of genius." (Cage's father had also been an inventor—of devices that could detect submarines.) In a 1982 interview that appeared in *The Observer* magazine, Cage recalled: "Schoenberg said I would never be able to compose, because I had no ear for music; and it's true that I don't hear the relationships of tonality and harmony. He said: 'You always come to a wall and you won't be able to go through.' I said, well then, I'll beat my head against that wall; and I quite literally began hitting things, and developed a music of percussion that involved noises."

As did Lou Harrison, Cage took inspiration from Henry Cowell in his pursuit of new sounds. The prepared piano, his logical extension of early experiments by Cowell, is one of his most productive inventions. By inserting objects—tacks, screws, and the like—into the strings, he transformed the instrument of genteel parlor and elite concert hall into a primitive, magical percussion orchestra. In subsequent years, Cage's palette expanded to include the entire world of sound, both manufactured and discovered. The 1942 *Credo in Us* is a good example; it uses piano, percussion, tin cans, gongs, and a combination of radio and phonograph in a wonderful kaleidoscope of sound from both modern technology and junkyard finds. Pianist Alan Feinberg characterizes the work as "a period piece that has outlasted its period. Its humor, rhythm, pathos, energy, playfulness, and simplicity delightfully reflect the composer we knew." Cage's journey led him to the most radical compositional statements in history (some of which will be examined in the next chapter).

A prepared piano.

While some composers, in particular Lou Harrison, thought of manufactured and discovered sound as aesthetically incompatible, others—John Cage the most prominent—discovered in them a creative energy, like that of a chemical reaction. Though composers such as Harrison and Cage draw from opposite ends of the material spectrum, they overlap in a crucial area: asserting the primacy of the individual artist's imagination over collective tradition, even over collective understanding, as George Antheil discovered. This is a maverick stance. And if, as in Antheil's case, we sometimes have to wait for the material means to catch up to the creative end, we can still admire its visionary power.

John Cage

(b. Los Angeles, California, September 5 1912; d. New York City, August 12 1992)

As a young man he left college to study music, art, and architecture in Europe. He painted and wrote poetry. He studied with Henry Cowell and Arnold Schoenberg before working as a dance accompanist in Seattle. There he began experimenting with percussion, found objects, and electronic instruments. Cage was a man who asked questions. What are we doing here? What are our expectations? Eager to eliminate subjectivity in composition, he went to the *I Ching* and threw coins to plan his pieces. With works such as the 1952 *4'33"*—four minutes and thirty-three seconds of silence "played" by a pianist merely sitting at a keyboard while the audience's coughs and whispers became the piece—he made listeners re-examine their assumptions. During the last forty years of his life his music was almost as much about philosophy and epistemology as it was about sound, and he outlined his principles in his influential book *Silence* (1961). To him, all sounds were music, and he attempted to break down the barriers between life and art.

chapter six

CONTROL AND BEYOND: The Postwar Avant-Garde

JOHN CAGE (II)

MORTON FELDMAN

EARLE BROWN

MILTON BABBITT

LUKAS FOSS

By the time the 20th century was half over, the character of Western society had changed character dramatically. The ebullience and sense of unlimited potential of the early years succumbed to the accumulating effects of economic depression, political extremism, and cultural nihilism that at last exploded in World War II and the Holocaust. Technology that had been hailed as a liberator became an oppressor, and the binding forces of faith and community dissolved, leaving disillusionment and rootlessness, whose common denominator was a loss of control. At the same time, however, ever more rapid developments in tools and transportation—tape recorders, television, jet planes, computers—continued to lend a seductive sense of motion and exhilaration. At mid-century, Americans accepted fundamental changes in the anchors of their world—space, time, and communication—and at the same time questioned their relevance.

Composers responded to the swirl of changes with some of the most dramatic aesthetic statements ever made. They explored extremes of creative expression. They explored questions of control and indeterminacy. At one pole, they let go, building the element of chance into performance and composition procedures. Leading figures in this exploration were the members of the "New York School": John Cage, Morton Feldman, Earle Brown. At the other end of the spectrum, composers were extending the principles of control beyond those specified by conventional notation to the minutest aspects of sound. Milton Babbitt, a mathematician as well as musician, and Lukas Foss made important contributions to this cultural dialogue.

CONTRIBUTORS TO THIS CHAPTER:
MICHAEL STEINBERG (CAGE, FELDMAN,
FOSS), JAMES M. KELLER (CAGE,
FELDMAN, BABBITT), AND SUSAN KEY
(BROWN, FOSS)

John Cage began his curious trek through life in Los Angeles and spent the last part of his life in New York City. The California-New York connection seems to surface frequently in music circles—perhaps because California roots engender an unusually unfettered sense of originality, and the artistic density of New York helps enrich that originality through close and constant contact with other creative types. But certain creators project such magnetism that like-minded souls flock to their sides, no matter where they are. Such was the case with Cage, whose career included stints in Paris, Seattle, and Chicago before he gravitated definitively to New York in the mid-1940s. That's where he gave his famous *Lecture on Nothing*, which employed the same rhythmic structure as Cage's musical compositions. One of the structural divisions involved the refrain, "If anyone is sleepy let him go to sleep" some fourteen times. Reportedly, at least one audience member was driven to distraction and ran out screaming. Later, Cage answered audience questions with one of six previously prepared answers without regard for the question—an extension of his Zen beliefs.

John Cage, Los Angeles, 1987.

An appreciation for Zen Buddhism led Cage to a study of the role that chance might play in the realization of music; accordingly, many of his mature works employ procedures regulated by directives derived by chance, at the spur of the moment, sometimes from the *I Ching*. He developed a penchant for leaving to fate not just the notes to be played but even the instruments employed in their execution. The music, he would argue, was already in place, just waiting to happen. As he wrote in his classic 1961 book, *Silence*, music was "simply a way to wake up to the very life we're living, which is so excellent once one gets one's mind and one's desires out of its way and lets it act of its own accord."

His most famous piece is one that contains, in the conventional sense, no music at all. *4'33"* consists of that amount of silence. Or "silence." David Tudor sat at a piano. That was it. The audience's shufflings and coughs and whispers were the piece, they and the noises inside listeners' heads as they searched for sense. There was a phenomenal virtuoso doing what—in some sense—any one of those listening could have done. (The "in some sense" is important because it would not be in the least interesting to have a non-pianist not playing a piano.) Cage wakes us up. What are we doing here? What are our expectations? What do we or are we expected to bring to the experience of listening? *4'33"* was self-destroying. Once an audience knew what was coming—or not coming— it was no longer a viable piece. That was typical Cage—in the age of the infinitely reproducible artwork (to borrow Walter Benjamin's phrase) to offer something that defied repetition.

Cage emanated a genial, somewhat child-like presence, a quality that can often shine through in his music. He once gave a lecture in which he had the sound manipulated electronically, distorted, chased through speakers that lined the four walls, so that one could not understand a word. Naturally, someone asked him why, since presumably he had something interesting to say, he had made it impossible for the audience to hear it. Cage's smile, then and always, was beatific: "It is to prepare you for your daily life." Detractors dismiss that aspect of his work as naïve (to wit Pierre Boulez's blunt assessment that "his freshness came from an absence of knowledge").

On the other hand, many musicians found liberation through his teachings and through performing his compositions, and the unveiling of his new works often stood as the highlight of adventurous music convocations. For a performer, the experience can be radical.

Cage offers a "Viewpoint" in response to a 1950 survey for a (never-published) *Dictionary of California Composers:* "Since music deals with sound, it deals with silence, only one of sound's characteristics, duration, measures both sound + silence therefor rhythmic (non harmonic) structure is in accord with nature of materials (<u>any</u> sounds + <u>any</u> silences)."

As Apo Hsu, conductor of one of the orchestras in the American Mavericks festival performance of *Dance/4 Orchestras,* says, "The intrigue in performing this music came not from the musical notes themselves, but in the 'nowness' of creating the moment. It was a feeling of Zen, 'be and let be.' For me, both the physical and mental settings were different from those in a 'normal' concert"—Hsu led one of four ensembles located in different parts of Davies Symphony Hall. "I had to connect within the immediate orchestra in front of me and outwards to three other orchestras that I couldn't see. There was a heightened sense of trust, spontaneity, and playfulness, which only exists in Cage's ingenious specific design. It was a wonderful feeling of artistic expression that's at once fresh, free, and communal." Conducting another of the orchestras, Peter Grunberg felt he was a player in a game that forced a re-ordering of conventional roles: The conductor assumed the role of instrumentalist (one of those who "realized" the score), the instrumentalists became instruments, and the listeners became score-readers. The experience, in sum, was more like chamber music than orchestral music.

Not everybody agreed that Cage's work constituted musical composition, and many even expressed reservations about Cage's music *per se*; still, he managed to prove interesting even to the most doctrinaire practitioners. Aaron Copland, who was certainly a composer of a very different stripe, wrote in 1973: "How one reacts to Cage's ideas seems to me largely to depend on one's own personal temperament. Those who envisage art as a bulwark against the irrationality of man's nature, as a monument to his constructive powers, will have no part of the Cageian aesthetic. But those who enjoy teetering on the edge of chaos will clearly be attracted." San Francisco Symphony percussionist Jack Van Geem expresses it thus: "The benefit we get from playing Cage is to underscore how we shouldn't become too ensconced in a particular style, structure, texture, or sound. He reminds you that music should feel fresh every time you create it."

Morton Feldman was our best inventor of charming and evocative musical titles before John Adams. Consider *Christian Wolff in Cambridge, Madame Press Died Last Week at Ninety, Routine Investigations, I Met Heine in the Rue Fürstenberg,* and *The Viola in My Life.* He was, of course, more. Those who have experienced his music will probably have recollections of pieces that are extremely quiet and quite long. His String Quartet No. 2 takes about five hours, which amounts to as much music as you will find in any Wagner opera, only there are no intermissions. As for the quiet, Feldman once remarked that his ideal audience consisted of dead people. Alan Feinberg puts it this way: "Performing Feldman's music can be like stepping into another universe where the musical events are low, magnified, surprising, and good for high blood pressure."

Feldman started in the usual way, playing piano as a child and trying his hand at composing. Later he studied with Wallingford Riegger and Stefan Wolpe, the latter one of the 20th century's most potent and unquenchably inventive musical personalities. He was also impressed, moved, and influenced by the music of Webern, his precursor in the art of *pianissimo* and cobweb textures, and the extremely different, rugged, aggressive Varèse. When Feldman died, he had been the Edgard Varèse Professor at the State University of New York at Buffalo since 1972, and his students there, he noted, tended to think of him as a cross between Wittgenstein and Zero Mostel. But the crucial encounter was the one with John Cage, which occurred in 1950. "The main influence from Cage was a green light," said Feldman. "It was permission, the freedom to do what I wanted."

What Feldman wanted was a divorce from Western musical tradition—from, as some members of the Cage circle occasionally liked to say, "what you people call music." More and more it became clear that his most intense intellectual and artistic investment was in painting, especially the work of the New York abstract expressionists, and he owned a sizable collection of works by Philip Guston, Jasper Johns, Franz Kline, Jackson Pollock, and Robert Rauschenberg. Several of his compositions are named for and dedicated to these artists and others. Guston, thirteen years older than himself, was something of a father figure to Feldman and hardly less influential than Cage. From Guston, he said, "I learned one had to make one's own morality. The material itself wasn't an intrinsic moral like sonata form. Guston made the 'I' the material. He showed me where the responsibility was—not to any 'style,' to any historical vested interest

From the score for Feldman's *Piece for 4 Pianos*. All four performers play the same part, at individual speeds.

Morton Feldman

(b. New York City, January 12 1926; d. Buffalo, New York, September 3 1987)

He studied composition with Wallingford Riegger and Stefan Wolpe but was most influenced by John Cage. During the 1950s in New York he associated with the composers Earle Brown and Christian Wolff; painters Mark Rothko, Philip Guston, Franz Kline, Jackson Pollock, and Robert Rauschenberg; and pianist David Tudor. His experiments in notation arose from an obsession to write music as he heard it, and what he created were works of delicate luminosity, slowly moving and defining silence. His later works tend to great length. His Second String Quartet (1983), for instance, lasts a little longer than *Götterdämmerung*.

of means." As Nils Vigeland has pointed out, Feldman sought to create in his own music "the sonorous equivalent of the 'flat surface' he admired in the American painters of his generation he knew so well, particularly in Mark Rothko and Philip Guston."

Often, Feldman left much in his music indeterminate, sometimes the pitches, more often duration of notes. (One of his associates recalled that whenever Feldman himself played the piano in an ensemble, he always finished last because he played slower than everyone else.) Feldman's works hover with a sense of immediacy, an almost physical presence that mirrors the effect a viewer might get from art by the composer's abstract-expressionist painter friends. From these visual artists Feldman borrowed the idea of conveying his messages through a sort of graphic notation, which he sometimes used to extend his expressive options beyond the traditional notes and rests of musical scores. Pianist Peter Grunberg, whose performance in *Piece for 4 Pianos* was his first encounter with Feldman, likened the performer's role to that in Baroque music, in which a performer fills in a large-scale harmonic canvas, and he comments: "It would be interesting to play this piece repeatedly in a concert program, in order to experiment with the listening experience—to play on the relationship between expectation and reality, which is so crucial to music."

Obviously, Feldman's most extreme pieces are not for everyone. Some find their purpose incomprehensible and their effect maddening; many, given both a technically exquisite and loving performance *and* an audience with good manners and the willingness to surrender to the experience, find them magically poetic. And Feldman did like to think of himself as a poet who worked with musical sounds. What many found engaging was the contrast between the delicacy of the music and the bulkiness of the person, and nearly everyone who ever had contact with him has a favorite story of some characteristic Feldman utterance, gnomic or drastically down to earth, given voice in intensely flavored Brooklynese. One of the most cherished experiences of his life was "walking along Eighth Street once in the late '60s, and one of those flower girls came over and said, 'You are our Schubert.'"

As his career advanced, one of the most striking features of Feldman's work was the slowness with which his music unrolls and, as a result, its great length. "My whole generation was hung up on the 20 to 25 minute piece," he wrote. "It was our clock. We all got to know it, and how to handle it. As soon as you leave the 20 to 25 minute piece behind, in a one-movement work, different problems arise. Up to one hour you think about form, but after an hour-and-a-half it's scale. Form is easy—just the division of things into parts. But scale is another matter. You have to have control of the piece—it requires a heightened kind of concentration. Before, my pieces were like objects; now, they're like evolving things."

Earle Brown with *Chef d'orchestra*, mobile by Alexander Calder, made expressly for *Calder Piece*.

Evolution is also central to the work of Earle Brown, whose compositions were inspired by the mobiles of Alexander Calder. Sounds are detached from the strictures of functional harmony and thus from the unidirectional force of temporal motion, seeming to float in time and space, gently transforming as, mobile-like, they turn and mingle. Brown experimented with open form and graphic notation, techniques intended to liberate music from conventional methods of control. He was drawn particularly to the question of how to achieve a balance of control and freedom. In his words, "There is no final solution to this paradox... which is why art is."

In keeping with his colleagues, Earle Brown's career path crossed the boundaries of music and other fields. Between his days as a jazz musician and those as a leading proponent of the avant-garde, Earle Brown studied engineering and mathematics at Northeastern University. Though he has lived and worked in Denver, Berkeley, and Baltimore, his reputation is most closely associated with fellow composers John Cage, Morton Feldman, and Christian Wolff in the New York School.

Another influence on Brown may seem surprising: American vernacular music. "You can't grow up in America and not have a connection to folk, jazz, or rock," he says. In describing his *Cross Sections and Color Fields* for a performance by the New World Symphony in the American Mavericks festival, Earle Brown reflected on both the vernacular and the visual influences in his work:

*As a young trumpet-playing jazz musician in the 1940s and '50s, I played in "territory"
Big Bands, and I very much admired the Big Band energy and sonorities of the Stan Kenton
orchestra and its composers and arrangers. (Morton Feldman called me "the lone arranger.")*
Cross Sections and Color Fields *is in no way an attempt to imitate or extend these
concepts—they already went further than I do here—but to be a kind of gentle "homage"
to that world that I enjoyed so much…. Having nothing to do directly (or does it?) with
the jazz background, my primary aesthetic influences were the spontaneity, direct contact,
the "now-ness," and the in-the-moment immediacy of the abstract expressionist painters—
especially the "improvisational" techniques of Jackson Pollock and the subtle coloristic effects
of Philip Guston and Bill deKooning. More than anything, in terms of* Cross Sections *and
many other works of mine, it was the example of the mobiles of Alexander Calder.*

*Since 1952 (after Calder), I have worked with aspects of "mobility" in the scoring and
performance of my work. There are many more radical applications of this principle in my
work, but I will try to give a reasonable explanation of* Cross Sections. *It is a closed form*

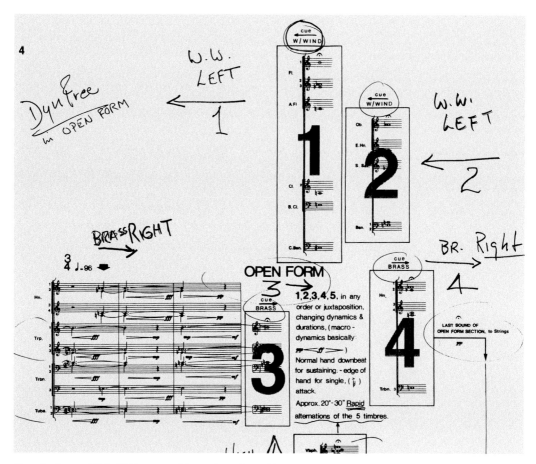

Cross Sections and Color Fields: score with conductor's markings.

Earle Brown

(b. Lunenburg, Massachusetts, December 26 1926)

He studied engineering and mathematics at Northeastern University before concentrating on music as a student at the Schillinger House School of Music. A follower of Jackson Pollock and Alexander Calder, he takes his cue from abstract impressionism—and some of his scores look like canvases ready to be framed. He introduced "open end" composition: The pages of the score can be arranged in any order, and each can be played upside down at will, aiming to involve the performer more actively as a co-creator of the composition. His approach: "to have elements exist in space,...the score being a picture of this space at one instant." In a sense his music is the aural equivalent of Calder's mobiles, free in form and never the same, though governed by its own special architecture.

(macro form determined by me) with mobile inner structures (form and continuity
and nuance determined by the conductor, based on my composed musical elements).
If, as I hope, you will hear this work more than once, you will clearly recognize the "work"
as Cross Sections and Color Fields, *by E.B., but also enjoy the poetic differences in*
the contributions of different conductors, or by the same conductor.

Brown's recent work continues his exploration of the boundaries between freedom and control. He describes his 1999 *SPECIAL EVENTS* for Cello and Piano as a continuation of his earlier compositional approach: "It is not an 'open-form' work, but has many 'open' sections where the two performers have a 'reservoir' of cello and piano material that I have written (no improvisation on their part); their musicality and imagination can be expressed with material that I have composed for them, but not **fixed**."

Exit indeterminacy; enter extreme control. A composer's best friend in achieving maximum control, as George Antheil and Conlon Nancarrow discovered earlier in the century, was technology. After World War II, composers received a boon in their handling of minute pitch gradations, thanks to the development of computer technology. The composer and one-time mathematician Milton Babbitt emerged as one of the most enthusiastic proponents of electronic music, which he began exploring in the mid-1950s with the RCA Mark II Synthesizer that resided at the Columbia-Princeton Electronic Music Studio in New York City. Musical traditionalists at that time, and for quite a while later, responded to computer music with sheer panic, but Babbitt showed in *Philomel* (1964) that electronic vs. acoustic music need not be an either/or proposition, that the two media could work in tandem to telling effect. Written for soprano Bethany Beardslee, *Philomel* is set to a poem by John Hollander and tells the tale, drawn from Ovid, of a hapless maiden—ravished, her tongue cut out—who turns into a melodious nightingale. The soprano is unquestionably the soloist here, but she's accompanied in this vocal and emotional tour-de-force by a four-track tape that mixes synthesized computer sounds with a modulated recording of her own voice.

For soprano Lauren Flanigan, singing *Philomel* was a revelation, beginning with the first rehearsal for her performance in the American Mavericks festival: "Was I insane when I said I could sing this? There is so much I don't know about this strange, wonderful, and elusive piece." Later, she reflected: "The lines, although melodically complex and extremely rangy, are like beautiful Schubert melodies when the intervals are condensed by dropping the octaves."

Milton Babbitt

(b. Philadelphia, Pennsylvania, May 10 1916)

He taught mathematics at Princeton before he joined its music faculty. Inaugurated electronic music programs at Princeton and Columbia. Expanded serial theory to encompass new ways of thinking about note values, dynamic levels, even instrumental color. Elaine Barkin and Martin Brody summarize in *The New Grove Dictionary of American Music*: "His emphasis on the relation between practice and theory, his insistence on the composer's assumption of responsibility for every musical event in a work, and his reinterpretation of the constituent elements of the Western musical tradition have had a vital influence on the thinking and music of numerous younger composers."

Writing on Babbitt for a concert in the San Francisco Symphony's New and Unusual Music series in 1984, Andrew Mead described the composer's approach to extending serialism's systemization of pitch to other musical elements. "His extensions and applications of twelve-tone structures are deeply involved with, and inspired by, the aural implications. All the subtle details of dynamics, articulation, and phrasing are carefully wrought to create perceivable associations among musical events. His music is not the result of a system, but his use of twelve-tone structures is the result of a passionate drive to compose music, a music that may be all that music can be. He has characterized himself on occasion as a 'maximalist composer.' Such an attitude towards composition has yielded a rich and beautiful music whose surface detail arises from deep underlying structures."

Babbitt shared one quality with his New York School colleagues: withdrawal from mainstream American musical life. His music, like theirs, struck many as too strange even to be considered music. In a famous article that ended up with the inflammatory headline, "Who Cares If You Listen?" (instead of the author's first choice, "The Composer as Specialist"), Babbitt likened musical composition to advanced science: "The time has passed when the normally well-educated man without special preparation could understand the most advanced work in, for example, mathematics, philosophy, and physics. Advanced music, to the extent that it reflects the knowledge and originality of the informed composer, scarcely can be expected to appear more intelligible than these arts and sciences to the person whose musical education usually has been even less extensive than his background in other fields."

Just to call Lukas Foss a composer is not to deal with him adequately. He is a prolific composer indeed, but also a conductor (of the Buffalo Philharmonic, the Milwaukee Symphony, and the Brooklyn Philharmonic, and everywhere a most innovative designer of programs), superb pianist, teacher, and fervent propagandist for a range of causes from avant-garde music to death-to-the-early-music-movement ("performance practice is for mediocrities"). Incurably and happily enthusiastic and inquisitive, he is better thought of as musician-at-large.

His was a cultivated Jewish family in Berlin, and he began very young to study piano and composition with Julius Goldstein. When Hitler came to power, the family fled to Paris, moving on to America in 1937. Lukas Foss's distinguished teachers include Isabelle Vengerova (piano), Rosario Scalero (composition), and Fritz Reiner (conducting) at the Curtis Institute, Serge Koussevitzky at Tanglewood, and, while Foss was a special student at Yale, Paul Hindemith. While on the faculty at UCLA, which he joined in 1953, Foss also was Music Director of the Ojai Festival; later, in Buffalo, he combined the music directorship of the Philharmonic with founding and running the Center for Creative and Performing Arts at the State University of

Lukas Foss

(b. Berlin, Germany, August 15 1922)

He came to this country at 15, when the Nazis made it impossible for his family to stay in Europe, and he became a persistent advocate of American music. He studied at the Curtis Institute and the Berkshire Music Center and as a conductor had two vastly different mentors, Fritz Reiner and Serge Koussevitzky. He is a pianist, teacher, and propagandist for new music. Has been music director of the Ojai Festival, Buffalo Philharmonic, Brooklyn Philharmonic, and Milwaukee Symphony. Has written in virtually all styles, from Romantic to neoclassical to avant-garde.

New York. Limitlessly energetic, cosmopolitan in background and outlook, never caught napping in the face of the new, Lukas Foss has cut a wide swath across America's musical scene ever since Robert Shaw introduced his Carl Sandburg cantata *The Prairie* in 1944.

Foss began as a composer of neoclassical music (that is a rough classification) and also of Americana such as *The Prairie*—a work well worth reviving—and an opera based on Mark Twain's *The Celebrated Jumping Frog of Calaveras County*. In 1956 he decided to include improvisation as part of the training for composers and performers at UCLA, and he founded what he called an Improvisation Chamber Ensemble with himself as pianist. This was both a symptom of a change in attitude as well as a stimulus and means to further change: "It changed me more than it changed my students." As a result, Foss entered upon a period of exploration in which his music covered the gamut from strict serialism to indeterminacy. Two of Foss's strongest and most performed works, *Time Cycle*—an innovative blend of literature, music, and philosophy— and *Echoi*, date from these years.

Time Cycle's texts are in the first person, though they communicate in very different terms. The first and fourth, by Auden and Nietzsche, are more abstractly philosophical; the inner movements, by Housman and Kafka, are more subjective. The constancy of an individual narra-

Lukas Foss in the 1970s.

tive stance throughout the change of language from English in the first two movements to German in the last two reverses Foss's own linguistic journey as an immigrant and produces a richer, more layered blend of word and sound—as though it represents a self that transcends superficial markers of identity. The use of serial procedures, different in each song, symbolizes the process of keeping time (a recurring cyclical pattern) as well as the human desire to control it. In the third movement the soprano begins a kind of incantation; the relatively longer text emphasizes the relationship between outer expression and inner emotion.

In her diary, soprano soloist Lauren Flanigan, who sang *Time Cycle* in the American Mavericks festival, expressed her emotions at the challenge of text and music in the third movement: "The third piece of the cycle, *Sechzehnter Januar*, eludes me. The pitch relationships and the counting and the speech. And KAFKA!!! Help!! The dilemma, the challenge and the triumph when it all comes together. It seems more and more that like the Babbitt, when you break these pitches down to their most basic intervallic relationships (2nds, 3rds, 5ths, whole and half steps instead of octave leaps and 9ths, etc.) you have Schubert and Brahms, and the true linear vocal beauty of these pieces and the beauty of intonation comes with this understanding."

When asked recently why he composed the piece for a soprano, Foss chuckled. "I love sopranos!"—revealing his playful attitude toward composition and why he never considered any of his techniques, including serialism, as stylistic determinants. He explains: "I believe that the more techniques I use, the richer is my vocabulary. What I call techniques is what many people call style. They say 'I'm a twelve-tone composer.' This is like Bach saying, 'I'm a fugue composer; I write nothing but fugues.' That would be ridiculous. Style is something totally different from technique.... The more techniques you use, the better."

Foss's refusal to be bound by stylistic labels is symbolic of an era in which there was no stylistic consensus. Not even the New York School was a school in the sense of following a common set of stylistic conventions. The developments in the postwar period both summarized and anticipated—they continued to probe earlier issues and yet reflected an intense search for new directions. At times it was difficult to distinguish the ongoing exploration of previous questions from movement ahead into uncharted territory—and, in truth, such directions are not always as distinct as we, in our quest for clarity, would like to think they are. No doubt history will judge many composers' efforts from this period as musical mannerism, fascinating dead ends. Yet neither is there any doubt that their bold conceptual gestures and brilliant, idiosyncratic productions will continue to work their peculiar brand of magic on all who approach music with open minds.

chapter seven

MIXED VOICES: The '60s Generation

TERRY RILEY

STEVE REICH

JOHN ADAMS

DAVID DEL TREDICI

MEREDITH MONK

FRANK ZAPPA

STEVEN MACKEY

After the anxious self-consciousness of the immediate postwar period, American culture in the '60s was pulled in two apparently contradictory directions: one, inner-directed, toward personal fulfillment; the other, outer-directed, toward collective social reform. The effect was to blur the line between public and private, and to strengthen the bonds that unite the inner and outer selves, individual and social identities. If the geographical and spiritual center of the earlier postwar avant-garde was New York, inspiration for much of the '60s culture emanated from California, where campus unrest spilled onto city streets and gave rise to the notion that "the personal is political."

The culture of the '60s gave a curious twist to the earlier artistic conflict between systematic control and open-ended freedom. The music departments of most universities had settled comfortably into the post-Schoenberg mode of academic formalism. Yet the young mavericks who came of adolescence in the postwar period—and those baby-boomers who followed on their heels—didn't define themselves in opposition to this or any other powerful status quo, as so many of their elders had done; they saw neither the need to conform nor to spend much energy rebelling. Pierre Boulez may have pronounced Schoenberg dead in 1951, but for this generation of Americans his status was not so much urgent as irrelevant.

CONTRIBUTORS TO THIS CHAPTER:
JOHN ADAMS (RILEY, ZAPPA),
K. ROBERT SCHWARZ (REICH),
MICHAEL STEINBERG (ADAMS,
DEL TREDICI), JAMES M. KELLER
(DEL TREDICI), PAUL ATTINELLO
AND SUSAN KEY (MONK), AND
STEVEN MACKEY (ON HIS MUSIC)

To judge by the number of masterpieces created, by the endurance of the movement, and by its popularity with both audiences and critics, the most significant musical trend to emerge in the '60s was minimalism. Some of its sources echo those of the postwar avant-garde: Certainly contemplation lies at the heart of Terry Riley's work, as it lies at the heart of Morton Feldman's. And just as Cage and many other 20th-century American composers had, Riley derived inspiration from the music and philosophy of Asia. In 1970 he traveled to India to study the singing of raga with Pran Nath; since the mid-1960s, Riley's works have tended more strongly away from notation and towards improvisation, with the composer evincing a seductive, melismatic style when playing either traditional keyboard instruments or synthesizers.

Riley's 1964 *In C*, a seminal work that Ed Ward, writing in *The Wall Street Journal*, called "as much a watershed as Stravinsky's *Rite of Spring* was in its day," dates from the years before Riley began his aesthetic journey to Asia. Riley made his initial mark on the music scene as a member of the first wave of the composers who came to be known as the minimalists. He had developed an interest in electronic music and avant-garde sounds as a member of the San Francisco Tape Music Study Center in the early 1960s; a few years later, while working in Paris at the ORTF recording studios, he crafted his signature sound of repeating sonic loops which, through multi-track manipulation, would go in and out of sync against the background of a steady rhythmic pulse. His *In C* still stands as the anthem of minimalism. Each of an undetermined number of players works his or her way through a sequence of fifty-three melodic motifs, repeating them at will, against the constant rhythmic pulse of a piano. *In C* was conceived as a work for accomplished musicians to interpret, but its materials actually lie within the reach of less skilled players.

In 1984, Riley joined members of the San Francisco Symphony for a concert in the Symphony's New and Unusual Music series, marking a 20th anniversary performance of *In C*. For that performance, John Adams, then the Symphony's Composer-in-Residence, provided comments on Riley and his music. "As a West Coast native," Adams wrote, Terry Riley "shares with members of the older generation like John Cage, Henry Cowell, Harry Partch, and Lou Harrison a distinctly open-minded attitude toward both the materials and organizational principles of composition.... Riley's real influences were from the popular American tradition: He played both the piano and saxophone in jazz groups from an early age, and much of the basis for his improvisational techniques was founded on the modal styles of the post-bop generation of saxophonists.

"...When it was recorded for Columbia Records in 1968, *In C* became an almost instantaneous success, even rivaling some rock records in sales. Riley became a cult figure for a time, and his second record for Columbia, *A Rainbow in Curved Air*, was also well received.... Riley's immersion in his studies with Pran Nath was so consuming—for ten years he worked daily for ten to twelve hours on mastering the subtleties of pitch and rhythmic structure that make the North Indian tradition one of the most refined and complex musical systems in the world—that he appeared to have dropped out of the avant-garde scene altogether. But the discipline gained in these traditional studies was also having a deep effect on his own creative work, both improvisational and composed, and during the '70s he performed both in his own style...and as a singer in the classical Indian raga style."

Riley's compositions have helped shape 20th-century American music, and they strongly influenced the works of Philip Glass, Steve Reich, and John Adams.

If Riley's *In C* marked minimalism's first major artistic statement, his younger contemporary Steve Reich's *Music for 18 Musicians* marked its acknowledgement as a potent artistic movement. *Music for 18 Musicians* (from here on we'll call it *18*) is not only one of Reich's greatest compositions, but one of a handful of late-20th-century works that can rightly claim to have altered the course of Western music. Reich himself admits that *18* marks a "high point" in his thirty-year career. "It's undoubtedly one of the best pieces I've ever done. Sometimes everything just comes together and suddenly you've created this wonderful organism, and in this piece it happened. That accounts for its durability—it has a real structural backbone, so it continues to please me twenty years later."

Although a bebop drummer as a teenager, Reich was a late bloomer when it came to composition. Not until after he received his bachelor's degree in philosophy did he decide to become a composer. Later, at Juilliard, he felt uneasy amid the shrill polemics of academe, which ignored the music he loved—such as the bebop of drummer Kenny Clarke or the modal jazz of John Coltrane. After three years at Juilliard, Reich left New York and went West in search of his compositional voice. At Mills College in Oakland, he studied with the Italian serialist Luciano Berio, who must have sensed Reich's acute discomfort with atonality. The advice Berio gave Reich was simple yet liberating: "If you want to write tonal music, why don't you *write* tonal music?"

Soon Reich would do precisely that. In the meantime, he plunged into the joyously chaotic San Francisco new-music world, which embraced everything from the music of Asia to the jazz of Coltrane, from a nascent rock scene to a Cageian delight in the sounds of the city. Reich had long been obsessed with taping the sounds he heard on San Francisco's streets (he even bugged the back seat of the taxi he drove). One day, while playing with two tape loops of the same speech fragment, he allowed them to slip out of alignment. As one crept ahead of the other, the two very gradually went out of sync (or out of "phase") and

Terry Riley

(b. Colfax, California, June 24 1935)

He studied with Robert Erickson at San Francisco State University and took a master's degree in composition from the University of California at Berkeley. He was an original member of the San Francisco Tape Music Center and in the early 1960s developed his unique method of repeating a phrase over a constant pulse. *In C* (1964) has been called as much a watershed as Stravinsky's *Rite of Spring* was in its day, and as the artist who introduced this manifesto of minimalism, Riley is spiritual ancestor to composers such as Steve Reich, Philip Glass, and John Adams. His influence has been also been felt on rock groups such as The Who and The Soft Machine.

then just as gradually realigned—although now the second loop was exactly one beat ahead of the first. While this process continued uninterruptedly, Reich realized he had stumbled upon a technique that could provide his proto-minimal music with a new kind of rhythmic structure.

And so arose not only his first mature composition, but the first to employ the musical process he called "phasing." *It's Gonna Rain* (1965) consists of only the title phrase, a melodious but apocalyptic utterance of a street preacher. The two tape loops start off in unison, incessantly repeating those three words, but soon one loop slowly slips out of phase. Eventually, as Reich layers up to eight tape loops of repeated speech fragments, all sorts of unforeseen acoustical combinations arise.

Although no fan of serialism's pulseless atonality, Reich admired its systematization. For him, music could not be completely satisfying unless it rested on a sturdy scaffolding. When he took his repetitive patterns and put them through the phasing process, what emerged was a slowly unfurling structure that was seamless, rigorous, and thoroughly audible. In 1968 Reich codified his minimalist aesthetic in a tersely worded essay called *Music as a Gradual Process.* Now the structure is synonymous with the music; the composition becomes the process of its unfolding. Soon Reich's music was tagged with the label "minimalism," a term he never liked. But this really was minimalist music. Restricted to a few ordered pitches, a uniform rhythmic pattern, a static tonal center, and a steady pulse, it consisted of nothing but repetition—transformed, of course, by the ongoing process of phasing. In typically relentless fashion, Reich remained fixated on phasing (and the procedures he derived from it) for several years.

Steve Reich and Musicians, performing *Music for 18 Musicians.*

But he could not continue down this austere and impersonal path indefinitely. A visit to Ghana resulted in his first masterpiece, a ninety-minute epic called *Drumming* (1971). The last part of *Drumming,* a joyous blend of drums, women's voices, marimbas, glockenspiels, piccolo, and whistling, proved that Reich was willing to compromise the clarity of the musical process—a primary tenet of minimalism—as long as he didn't deviate from its structure. Now the doors were flung open to a vastly enriched timbral universe. In *Six Pianos* and *Music for Mallet Instruments,*

Steve Reich

(b. New York City, October 3 1936)

A founder of minimalism, he took a degree in philosophy from Cornell, then studied composition with Hall Overton and at Mills College in Oakland, California with Darius Milhaud and Luciano Berio. At Mills, he became interested in Asian and African music, then went on to study drumming at the University of Ghana and Balinese gamelan with teachers in Seattle and Berkeley. He also studied Hebrew cantillation. Reich introduced the concept of phasing, "a form of counterpoint produced when two or more instruments play identical repeated material at a given time delay" (in John Adams's succinct summation). He has produced a body of work that has consistently won the ears of audiences and the approbation of critics. Since the late 1960s, he has been an influence not just on concert music, but on rock. Lately, he has explored the boundaries of multi-media art, and with videographer Beryl Korot he has created documentary video theater pieces such as *The Cave* (1993) and *Hindenburg* (1998).

Steve Reich and Beryl Korot's *Hindenburg* combines live performance and video.

Voices and Organ (both works from 1973), he renounced tonal stasis and introduced several juxtapositions of key, and in the latter work he embraced the lush timbres of the Balinese gamelan (which he studied in 1973 and 1974).

When Reich looked back on *18* from a distance of two decades, he noted its roots in tradition. "The thing about *18* is that it's both several steps forward and several steps backward—back into more recognizable Western phenomena, [such as] the world of harmony, the world of careful orchestration, which came together here for the first time. Aspects of *18* reappear in the opening measures of *Sextet, The Desert Music,* and *New York Counterpoint,* not to mention a type of scat-singing—which, by the way, definitely comes from Ella Fitzgerald." But what makes *18* unprecedented is the expansion of Reich's previously static harmonic language.

In an unusually candid 1977 interview with English composer Michael Nyman, Reich talked about his changed aesthetic. No longer would the work be based on a single, gradual process; no longer would the process be audible, even sacrosanct; no longer was the act of composition impersonal. The bare-bones austerity of minimalism had become the stuff of history:

> *There was a didactic quality to the early pieces, and looking back I'd say that, when you discover a new idea, it's very important to present that idea in a very forceful and clear and pared-down way.... But once you've done that, what do you do? Just sit there cranking out one perfect phase piece after another? Personally, as a human being, I feel the need to move on, not to sell out or cop out, but just to move on.*

Minimalism had met with success, and that success was not lost on the mainstream press. A *Time* magazine article in 1982 marked the first mention of the style in the major media. Under the headline "The Heart is Back in the Game," the article profiled Riley, Reich, LaMonte Young, Philip Glass, and John Adams, characterizing minimalism as "directly emotional in its appeal, a deliberate rebuke to three decades of arid, overly intellectualized music produced by the postwar avant-garde."

Time described John Adams as "the fastest-rising minimalist composer—and potentially the most influential of all." Only three years later, Adams bounded onto the Davies Symphony Hall stage to acknowledge the tumultuous applause that greeted the premiere of *Harmonielehre*. While he had been an enlivening presence on the Bay Area musical scene for some time, he was just beginning to be known nationally as an interesting "younger" composer.

Like Reich, Adams used systematic procedures as a stimulus to self-discovery and a manner of moving beyond avant-garde academic training. Recently he reflected on his aesthetic process in creating his 1978 *Shaker Loops*:

> Shaker Loops *began as a string quartet entitled* Wavemaker. *At the time, like many a young composer, I was essentially unaware of the nature of those musical materials I had chosen for my tools. Having experienced a few of the seminal pieces of American minimalism during the early 1970s, I thought their combination of stripped-down harmonic and rhythmic discourse might be just the ticket for my own unformed yearnings. I gradually developed a scheme for composing that was partly indebted to the repetitive procedures of minimalism and partly an outgrowth of my interest in waveforms. The "waves" of* Wavemaker *were to be long sequences of oscillating melodic cells that created a rippling, shimmering complex of patterns like the surface of a slightly agitated pond or lake. But my technique lagged behind my inspiration, and this rippling pond very quickly went dry.* Wavemaker *crashed and burned at its first performance. The need for a larger, thicker ensemble and for a more flexible, less theory-bound means of composing became very apparent.*

> *Fortunately, I had in my students at the San Francisco Conservatory of Music a working laboratory to try out new ideas, and with the original* Wavemaker *scrapped, I worked over the next four months to pick up the pieces and start over. I held on to the idea of the oscillating patterns and made an overall structure that could embrace much more variety and emotional range. Most importantly, the quartet became a septet, thereby adding a sonic mass and the potential for more acoustical power. The "loops" idea was a technique from the era of tape music, where small lengths of prerecorded*

tape attached end-to-end could repeat melodic or rhythmic figures ad infinitum. (Steve Reich's It's Gonna Rain *is the paradigm of this technique.) The Shakers got into the act partly as a pun on the musical term "to shake," meaning either to make a tremolo with the bow across the string or else to trill rapidly from one note to another.*

The flip side of the pun was suggested by my own childhood memories of growing up not far from a defunct Shaker colony near Canterbury, New Hampshire. Although, as has since been pointed out to me, the term "Shaker" itself is derogatory, it nevertheless summons the vision of these otherwise pious and industrious souls caught up in the ecstatic frenzy of a dance that culminated in an epiphany of physical and spiritual transcendence. This dynamic, almost electrically charged element, so out of place in the orderly mechanistic universe of minimalism, gave the music its raison d'être and ultimately led to the full realization of the piece.

Harmonium, composed for the San Francisco Symphony in 1981, though still diatonic and essentially consonant, is looser in language than the preceding *Phrygian Gates, Shaker Loops,* and *Common Tones in Simple Time.* It has a quicker rate of harmonic change and more dramatic contrast, and it was at the time of completing *Harmonium* that Adams described himself as "a minimalist who is bored with minimalism." Impetus for another renewal came from listening to Wagner. "I was thunderstruck by the simplicity and power of the emotions. I knew all at once that I wanted to move toward this intense emotionality in my own music."

Yet it is one thing for an artist to know that it is time to move and quite another to discover where and how to move. Adams found himself deeply mired in a crisis of language. For a whole year he could keep nothing he wrote. He abandoned a project for the Santa Fe Chamber Music Festival, and he made what seemed like an unending series of false starts during the first eight months of work on a new San Francisco Symphony commission for a symphony. It looked doubtful that the premiere could take place as scheduled. Then, one night, Adams had a dream in which, as he told Jonathan Cott in an interview, he saw himself "driving across the... [San Francisco-Oakland] Bay Bridge, and looking out saw a huge tanker in the bay. It was an image of immense power and gravity and mass. And while I was observing the tanker, it suddenly took off like a rocket ship with an enormous force of levitation. As it rose out of the water, I could see a beautiful brownish-orange oxide on the bottom part of its hull. When I woke up the next morning, the image of those huge [E minor chords with which *Harmonielehre* begins] came to me, and the piece was off like an explosion."

John Adams

(b. Worcester, Massachusetts, February 15 1947)

After taking a degree at Harvard, where he studied
with Leon Kirchner, he settled in San Francisco.
There he led a new-music ensemble at the
San Francisco Conservatory of Music. In 1979
he became the San Francisco Symphony's first
Composer-in-Residence, a post he occupied until
1985, and during this time he established his
reputation with the concert works *Harmonium*
(1981) and *Harmonielehre* (1985), in which he
moved away from the minimalist style of his
earlier music. He tackled contemporary history
in his operas *Nixon in China* and *The Death of
Klinghoffer*, and by century's end he had become
America's most-performed living composer.

The Maverick and the Orchestra: An Exchange

BILL BENNETT:

The traditional orchestra still has the power to delight, and it often does so by absorbing sounds from outside the concert hall (witness Lou Harrison's music), but it has lost its power to speak for today's mass audience (the way that Copland did in his day) and it may have lost the power to shock. That role was taken over long ago by other art forms, most notably film and television, but also by jazz and rock, especially during the early years of those popular idioms.

Given that, it's not surprising that so many composers have opted to incorporate electronic instruments into their music, or have eschewed the front-and-center use of a "classical" orchestra in favor of more "popular" instruments or ensembles (Duke Ellington and Steve Reich come to mind). Even John Adams, who writes ravishing music for large orchestra, makes electronic instruments an integral part of his scores and is clearly influenced by synthesizers and sequencers.

In turn, the use of machines and other, non-classical musical idioms necessarily influences the musical structures that showcase those instruments. The ultimate effect of these trends, all of them presaged by George Antheil, may be quite pleasant for the listener, but it may not be good for the future of our institution.

"But if we play all these American things, what's to become of Mozart and Boccherini?"

Drawing by George Hager

From *Musical America*, May 25, 1937.

I play the oboe, an instrument with a soulful and somewhat introspective voice, one of the oldest members of the orchestra and an instrument that hasn't been associated with a maverick tradition in a long, long time. The oboe can't compete with an electric guitar or a trap set, much less a trumpet or trombone; the oboe can't play endless streams of repeated eighth notes, like a drum machine, or endless arpeggios, like a sequencer. It's not very adept at free flights of improvisation. What the oboe does very well is play beautiful, vocal sounds in a limited range. It's ideal for gorgeous melodies played alone or with minimal accompaniment.

I would have never taken up the oboe if it weren't for the rich and melodic solo lines I heard on records and at concerts as a child. All of that material was written by composers who I thought cared about the classical orchestra and its traditions. With the exception of Copland, there wasn't one composer represented in the American Mavericks festival who would have inspired me to take up my instrument again. Is that a good thing?

I understand that we often need perspective on old traditions. But I wonder whether the maverick tradition, as we defined it, is pointing us in the right direction? Or do we do ourselves a disservice by endorsing that spirit?

JOHN ADAMS — A RESPONSE TO BILL BENNETT:

I grew up playing the clarinet. My father was my first teacher. He had played it during the 1930s and '40s, when Benny Goodman and Artie Shaw were the pop culture stars of their day. By the time I got to college the electric guitar and heavily amplified rock music had replaced big band swing, and the clarinet was a ludicrously old-fashioned instrument. Paul McCartney used it in a song about retired people to set the tone for "When I'm Sixty-Four." Grace Slick held an old metal clarinet in her lap for the cover of the Jefferson Airplane's *Surrealistic Pillow*. By then it had become little more than a tchotchke. But there was no clarinet on any of her songs, and none I remember on any of the other great albums from that era. Imagine: I thought my life in music was already foreclosed due to an error in the instrument I'd chosen at a very young age. I felt the same sort wistfulness and chagrin that Bill Bennett gives voice to. But thirty years later, the clarinet is still around, and it has reappeared as an important instrument in styles I never would have imagined back in the 1960s. Not only has it found its way into the most progressive of avant-garde jazz, but its ethnic roots are being unearthed with remarkable results. Who could have predicted that klezmer music would take hold with such strength and that it would provide a new route of expression for young composers? The Argentinian composer Osvaldo Golijov, one of the true bright lights among new composers, several years ago wrote an astonishing piece called *The Dreams and Visions of Isaac the Blind* for klezmer clarinet and string quartet. When I heard it a few years back in a performance by David Krakauer and the Kronos Quartet, I thought I'd stepped into a new terrain of expressiveness, and it was all because of this new style of writing for the clarinet.

I mention this example because it is for me a cautionary tale about the unpredictability of musical tastes and styles. Bill assumes that his oboe, with its fundamentally lyric qualities, lacks the power or the mechanical precision to play a significant role in contemporary music of the kind we heard in the American Mavericks festival. That may be true for the moment. But let's keep him away from the pawn shop — the only thing we know about the future is that it is bound to surprise us. Bill looks at the repertory of the Mavericks festival and intuits that all the qualities he has to offer have little place in current musical language. But wait a minute. Ten years from now, there is guaranteed to be a new way of experiencing music. There is no doubt that things will change, and it's likely to be radical change, not a slow, even progression. Just look at what went on in the 20th century. When unalloyed dissonance seemed to be the rage, it was answered in the following generation by emphatic consonance. One year's fetish for complexity was overturned the following year by a move toward extreme simplicity. Last year was loud. Next year is likely to be so soft you'll barely hear it. When people ask me what is going to happen to new music in the next twenty or fifty years, I tell them that I could no more predict that than Edward Elgar could have predicted the electric guitar.

The problem with Bill Bennett's oboe is that he plays the classics on it with such consummate expressiveness and imagination that we tend to think this is what the instrument was made for — to play Beethoven and Schubert. But viewed less romantically, as a raw source of sound and emotion, Bill and his oboe could very well be the springboard for a whole new literature. Yes, maybe the next breed of oboe-hero will come with a personal amplifier, a computer, spiked hair and significant piercing, but still it will be something unexpected and, for the moment anyway, unimaginable. ❭

For three months Adams worked like a man possessed. It sounds unbearably corny, but Adams had found his future by looking into the past. A musician of wide culture, he has never expressed disdain for the central tradition of Western music. "I don't try to turn my back aggressively on the past," he says. "I try to embrace it."

Adams has produced some of his most significant works for musical theater—not surprising for a composer who describes his music as "more pictorial or cinematographic than it is developmental." His 1987 opera *Nixon in China* used the individuals and events of contemporary politics to create a powerful drama of human archetypes. Four years later *The Death of Klinghoffer* took on an even more daunting subject: the hijacking of the cruise liner *Achille Lauro* by Palestinian terrorists and their assassination of a handicapped American Jew. Adams turned to the sights and sounds of the American vernacular for *I Was Looking at the Ceiling and Then I Saw the Sky*, a love story set in inner-city Los Angeles amidst contemporary racial and social conflicts.

Riley, Reich, Adams: All three of these minimalist composers continue to move in new directions, both expanding and rendering problematic the stylistic term itself. Riley continues to explore the connections between Indian music and American vernacular styles. His piano concerto, premiered with the Paul Dresher Ensemble in February 2001, incorporates raga-like scales, boogie-woogie, blues, and "sweet jazz" sounds in an exhilarating

John Adams conducts the New World Symphony in his *Shaker Loops*, at the American Mavericks festival.

kaleidoscope. Steve Reich is currently working with video artist Beryl Korot on a new fusion of eye and ear. The latest effort is *Three Tales*, A Documentary Video Opera. *Three Tales* is about three significant events from the early, middle and late 20th century: the *Hindenburg* disaster, the explosion of the first atom bomb over the Bikini Atoll, and the first cloned sheep, Dolly. Each tale reflects on the growth and implications of technology during the 20th century—physical, ethnical, religious, and spiritual. John Adams's latest work returns to his collaborations with stage director Peter Sellars. Their multimedia oratorio *El Niño* (2001) is a retelling of the Nativity story with a libretto culled from Hispanic poets and the Gnostic gospels. It is the most cogent statement to date of the assumption underlying all of Adams's work: that music can be not only topical, but spiritually enriching and beautiful.

In such company, David Del Tredici seems perhaps less radical a figure, but his originality is distinctive and striking in its own right. As with all of the maverick composers, his output reflects a degree of obsessive inquiry into sources of inspiration that resonate with personal ferocity. While Del Tredici was still a student, an unhappy encounter with a teacher at Aspen made him want to give up piano. He went on to write a piano piece, *Soliloquy*, and showed it to Darius Milhaud. The veteran master's response was succinct: "My boy, you are a composer." Del Tredici counts these as the six most important words ever spoken to him. He holds degrees from University of California at Berkeley and Princeton, and among his teachers were Arnold Elston, Earl Kim, Seymour Shifrin, and Roger Sessions. Crucial, as well, was the support of Aaron Copland, who saw to it that he got a scholarship to the Berkshire Music Center at Tanglewood and who later, as conductor, introduced his work in Europe. Del Tredici counts Copland and Leon Kirchner among the powerful musical and personal influences of his life.

The works that first attracted attention to him, *I Hear an Army*, *Night Conjure-Verse*, and *Syzygy*, are all settings of James Joyce. But beginning in 1968 and continuing for eighteen years, he hung virtually all his compositions on the writings of Lewis Carroll. His involvement, he says, began with his discovery of Martin Gardner's *The Annotated Alice*, particularly with the information that most of the poems in the Alice books are parodies of poems or popular songs known to Carroll's contemporary readers but, beyond the fact that Carroll chose to parody them, forgotten today. "The idea of setting to music these Carrollian poem-parodies struck fire in my imagination and led me to compose a whole series of pieces, each independent, but each based on different episodes from the book: *Pop-Pourri* (1968), *Lobster-Quadrille* (1969), *Vintage Alice* (1972), *Adventures Underground*

(1973), *In Wonderland* (1974), *Final Alice* (1975), *Illustrated Alice* (1976), *In Memory of a Summer Day* (1980), *Happy Voices* (1980), *All in the Golden Afternoon* (1981), *Quaint Events* (1981), and *Haddocks' Eyes* (1986).

As his *Alice* series began to unfold, Del Tredici's language underwent a drastic change. It used to be dissonant and atonal, he told James Wierzbicki, author of the Del Tredici entry in *The New Grove Dictionary of American Music*. But, he said, "I couldn't imagine setting a Carroll text to dissonant music. Dissonant music can't possibly project the mood that surrounds Carroll's writing. In order to create that mood I had to rethink everything I had done up to that time. I had to think about tonality again, not because I was trying to bring back the music of an older period, but because I just had to invent things in that language."

What is it about Lewis Carroll that hooked Del Tredici? In part, he explained in an interview with the conductor Richard Dufallo, it was the appeal of nonsense texts. "With nonsense," he said, "I felt somehow I could do whatever I wanted with the words. When I began to set the *Alice in Wonderland* texts, I took the craziest ones first, like 'Jabberwocky,' because they were, in a sense, the most adaptable to my atonal language.... There is no expectation or tradition for setting nonsense verse. It was very liberating. As I went on with the *Alice* pieces, *An Alice Symphony*, *Adventures Underground*, I think the most seriously tonal might have been *Vintage Alice*.... I certainly wasn't tonal in the Bach-Beethoven-Brahms sense. But I was beginning to get a feel for tonal materials."

Del Tredici's setting of "The Mouse's Tail," with the notes tracing the shape of the subject.

Still, Del Tredici insisted that the text never gave him a shape for his compositions, but rather an idea—nothing more. "For example," he continued, "in *Adventures Underground* I set the poem 'The Mouse's Tail.' What's remarkable about the poem is that it appears on the page in the shape of a tail. It starts at the top of the page with very thick letters and gradually winds down to the bottom with the tiniest print available. Very original. I thought, well, to set such a special-looking poem, I should make each page of music also look special—like a tail. I spent a lot of time figuring out how it would sound. An audience after all can't *hear* a tail! So it must look like a tail and yet sound like music. Again, it was the kind of restriction which excites my imagination. And it yielded a whole brave new world of musical sound that I would not otherwise have gotten."

David Del Tredici

(b. Cloverdale, California, March 16 1937)

He grew up in a small town north of San

Francisco, studying piano with Bernhard

Abramowitsch in Berkeley and Robert Helps

in New York. Twice he was soloist with the

San Francisco Symphony, playing Mendelssohn

with Enrique Jordá and Saint-Saëns with Arthur

Fiedler. *Happy Voices*, commissioned by the

San Francisco Symphony, was introduced at

the opening of Davies Symphony Hall in 1980,

the year another of his works, *In Memory of*

a Summer Day, was awarded the Pulitzer Prize.

Another Symphony commission, *Gay Life*, was

introduced in the spring of 2001. In composition,

he started out as a "modernist" but discovered

his unique identity in a series of tone pictures

based on *Alice in Wonderland*—music in which,

says the lexicographer Nicolas Slonimsky, he

projected "overt tonal proclamations, fanfares,

and pretty tunes that were almost embarrassingly

attractive, becoming melodiouser and harmo-

niouser with each consequent tone portrait

of Alice."

Gay Life, Del Tredici's most recent work, continues his musical involvement with poetry. This time, however, Del Tredici turns his attention to other inspirations that he finds personally compelling, particularly to American poetry and to matters relating to gay consciousness. "My latest creative impulse," he writes, "is toward wholeness—revealing my personal life in my music."

Another artist who draws inspiration from the expressive potential of the voice is Meredith Monk. Trained in an interdisciplinary performing arts program at Sarah Lawrence College, with time spent at the MacDowell Colony, Monk is alive to the ways separate art forms enrich each other. Unlike most modern music—indeed, unlike most Western music of any period—Monk's tunes, canons, and subtle melodic variations are rooted in the body, in dance and gesture, heartbeat and pulse. Monk was considered a choreographer when she first appeared on the scene in the mid-1960s; her early schooling had included eurhythmics, an educational combination of movement and dance. Probably that early experience helped her to understand her remarkable voice, even after classical training, as an extension of physical movement, and her music as a direct expression of the dreams of the body rather than of the mind.

Monk's gracefully powerful voice and poised, complex stage presence make her the most effective interpreter of her own music. But even performed by others, Monk's music is alive, memorable, seductively immediate. Its relatively

Meredith Monk and her ensemble join members of the San Francisco Symphony Chorus in music from *ATLAS*.

simple parameters account for this, as do its vivid chords and patterns. In Monk's work, we hear the human voice purring, weeping, yelling; we hear it throughout its vast range of possible inflections, rather than limited to the classical diatonic pitches and consistent tone learned by imitating keyed wind instruments. Monk's vocalizations are said to have been influenced by Native American, Balkan, or even Tibetan techniques; but she has pointed out that she developed most of her techniques before she ever heard such musics. As she has suggested, you can create music in all the styles of the world if you can ignore the learned restrictions imposed by quasi-instrumental training and Mozartian vocal ideals.

Meredith Monk

(b. Lima, Peru, November 20 1943)

Born in Peru while her pop singer mother was on tour, she grew up in New York and Connecticut. After taking a degree from Sarah Lawrence College she embarked on a career of composition, filmmaking, and directing. In her widely acclaimed music-theater pieces, she explores the possibilities of the human voice, melding ensembles in wordless choruses that evoke almost trance-like effects. In 1978 she formed the chamber group Meredith Monk and Vocal Ensemble. Her award-winning films include *Ellis Island* (1981), and in 1991 she unveiled her full-length opera *ATLAS*.

Even within Western cultural boundaries, Monk frustrates classification. It is difficult at times to say if her works are more like "classical" or "folk" music, or whether they owe more to minimalism or noise composition. Much of her music, including practically all of the keyboard music, could indeed be called "process" music; the music unfolds through repetition, proceeding with attractive patterns that repeat in a consistently unexpected but perfectly natural manner.

So why is Meredith Monk's music rarely heard, aside from performances by her own small circle? This is where the utopian aspects of her imagination hit a real-world snag, because our musical culture operates chiefly by notation, through the transmittal of musical information in scores. Monk has always resisted notating her music. Some of the early works, such as *Key*, *Tablet*, and *Dolmen Music*, exist in spare but careful scores—unpublished, and created apparently for copyright purposes. Other major works, such as *The Games* and *Quarry*, exist as a handful of sketches used by the members of Monk's group as mnemonics. Nurit Tilles, a classically trained pianist who works with Monk, says she had a difficult time learning the music at first because there was no score to memorize, no concrete abstraction of the work at hand. Instead, the music grew and changed in rehearsal, gradually developing into something dense and multi-layered.

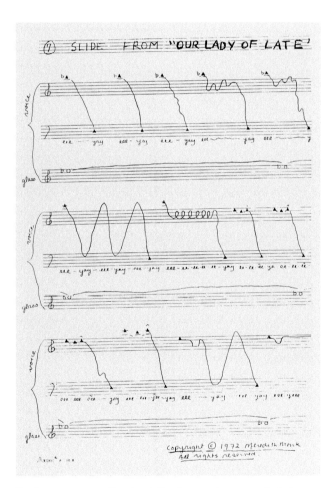

Monk uses unconventional notational means to communicate her unconventional vocal techniques.

In the late 1980s, one of Monk's group, Wayne Hankin, began suggesting that she notate more of her music. The chance came with the opera *ATLAS*, which had to be written out for a chamber orchestra and for singers who had just begun working with Monk. *ATLAS* is based on the writings of explorer Alexandra David-Néel, and it tells the story of a woman named Alexandra Daniels, whose passion for spiritual self-discovery takes her from small-town America to the ends of the earth and beyond. The single, almost simple plot ties together a remarkable array of imaginative scenes and characters as Alexandra and her traveling companions encounter beings both kindly and threatening.

The *ATLAS* score, though notated, cannot convey certain vocal sounds because Western notation is weak when it comes to timbre or inflection, both of which are major elements in Monk's music. Monk herself is dissatisfied with scores, calling them "misleading"; this is understandable, as the subtle process of bringing meaning to a musical score ("performance practice") is difficult to learn. Given that Monk's music is distinct from the usual vocal fare, it is no wonder she worries that notes on a page won't convey that distinction. A performer might *read* all the notes correctly and still not *sing* the piece. San Francisco Symphony Chorus Director Vance George agrees: "It's not like reading a page of music; it really does have to be internalized. The singers must learn to be energetic and relatively free within the confines of an overall shape and pattern. It was a long process to get the [San Francisco Symphony Chorus] singers attuned to her particularity; the slightest entrance that is early, late, flat, or sharp is thrown into bold relief against the minimalist premise of her music."

"I've always thought of the voice as a language itself," says Monk. "So if I hear English at the same time as I hear the voice, I think of that as two languages. If I do use language…it's as much a sound texture as it is a text.… If I do use text, it will be very simple, and it will be there as much for the sound of it as for the meaning. I also think that music, itself, is such an evocative medium. It's very openhearted. And I don't like the idea that people have to work through the screen of language." The result is a pure, almost pre-linguistic expression, simultaneously a traditional mode of communicating language and a transcendence of that mode. Although her primary work has been with voice, Monk is exploring the idea of writing a piece for symphony orchestra.

Frank Zappa was a self-taught musician who created an uncontested niche for himself in the country's culture and maintained it for more than thirty years with a mixture of irony, satire, instrumental virtuosity, creative experimentation, and shrewd business acumen. Zappa was to music what Mark Twain and H.L. Mencken were to literature. His life was so intensely lived, so diverse in its accomplishments, and so socially provocative that any attempt to summarize would only be a fool's mission. What other American composer had his music recorded by Pierre Boulez, went head to head with Tipper Gore over censorship of lyrics, and even ran for President? What rock star ended his career by producing (at his own expense) recordings of the complete ensemble music of Edgard Varèse? Who wrote the pop classic *Don't Eat the Yellow Snow* as well as a fiendishly complex orchestral composition called *Penis Dimension*?

Another title by Zappa, *Bogus Pomp*, more or less describes his attitude toward conventional "classical" music and the traditional way of presenting it. As someone who had grown up during the 1950s on the outskirts of Los Angeles, Zappa brought an outsider's vision to the world of concert music. An enormously complex artist with huge ambitions and a workaholic's energy, Zappa was 14 when he first heard the music of Varèse. The effect of this exposure, and in particular his encounter with Varèse's compositions for percussion, stayed with Zappa for the rest of his life. Despite his lack of formal training in composition, he began writing his own style of "new music" in the early 1960s, just before his first albums with his band, The Mothers of Invention, were making his name a household word. Albums such as *Freak Out!* and *Uncle Meat*, products of the psychedelic era, showed a restless compositional mind incessantly looking for fresh ways of saying otherwise familiar things. His songs, laced with pungent satire and parody, were cast in a musical language that went far beyond the generic sound of contemporary rock. He began to use the mixing studio as a creative tool well before *Sergeant Pepper* made the concept of the studio-produced album an established artistic entity. During the late 1960s Zappa compositions featured instrumental combinations and weirdly astonishing tape-mixing techniques that seemed every bit as provocative and revolutionary as anything being done at the time by Berio, Cage, or Stockhausen. The difference, of course, was that the tone of Zappa's work was always one of sharp parody. The context was usually that of a satire of lowbrow suburban life or bitterly funny take-offs on Zappa's lifelong bete-noire, the commercial pop music industry. Zappa was "in your face" years before the term became a commonplace in our lives.

Zappa wrote concert music with the same zeal he brought to producing his rock records and running his production company. Cut loose from the regular pulsation of rock, the language in his orchestral works was polymorphous and unpredictable, often employing rhythmic groupings that were (and still are) extremely difficult to realize. The titles are pure Zappa: *Mo and Herb's Vacation, The Girl in the Magnesium Dress, G Spot Tornado, Get Whitey.*

In 1983, a commission from Pierre Boulez and the Ensemble Intercontemporain resulted in a recording of orchestral works conducted by Boulez himself, along with compositions realized on the synclavier. This was not Zappa's first collaboration with the classical establishment. Not long before, he had hired the London Symphony Orchestra to record an album of his orchestral works, conducted by Kent Nagano. The experience of having to work within the time constraints of a modern symphony orchestra frustrated him, and not until the last few years of his life did he find the kind of willing and able collaborators he desired in the players of the Ensemble Modern in Frankfurt. With them Zappa was able to establish the kind of productive and unconstrained working relationship that would feed his

Frank Zappa

(b. Baltimore, Maryland, December 21 1940; d. Los Angeles, California, December 4 1993)

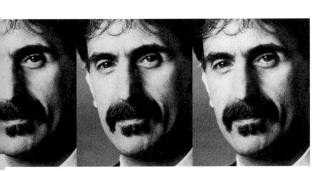

Zappa's official biography is simple—"American composer. fl. 1940-1993"—and suggests that describing the man is as difficult as categorizing his music. As a rock musician, he is a counter-culture icon—leader of The Mothers of Invention, the Zappa of the film *200 Motels* and the albums *Hot Rats*, *Weasels Ripped My Flesh*, and *Burnt Weeny Sandwich*. But he also composed for orchestra—theme following theme in free succession, à la Varèse—and he conducted the San Francisco Contemporary Music Ensemble and Berkeley Symphony. Pierre Boulez commissioned music from him and recorded an album of his works, *The Perfect Stranger*. Zappa used tape collage, fused rock and jazz, demanded virtuosity of his players, and disdained those who equate Good Taste with Great Art.

particular mode of creative thought. Commissioned by the Ensemble Modern, Zappa created an evening-length event, *The Yellow Shark*, that presents the quirky genius of his orchestral imagination at its best.

Dupree's Paradise is the more successful of the two compositions created for the Boulez sessions. Named for a night-spot in the San Fernando Valley, it was drawn from an earlier sketch and put into final form for the Ensemble Intercontemporain in Paris. The beginning and ending utilizes similar "con brio" material, a series of simple, repeated figures in the brass and winds, and it makes use of the stereophonic seating of the orchestra (all instruments come in stereo pairs, even the grand pianos). In between these passages of almost sitcom cheerfulness are longer sections of denser, more tonally ambivalent material. The various instrumental families often group themselves homophonically, at times reminding one of the iterating bird patterns in Messiaen's music. The piece is typical of Zappa's orchestral compositions in its combining of avant-garde techniques with parodies of generic commercial music. The final bars with their harp glissandi and rising brass figures could fit effortlessly into your favorite *Leave it to Beaver* episode.

Leave it to Beaver, curiously, makes a good transition to baby-boomer Steve Mackey. When asked about the connection, he notes that "*Leave it to Beaver* was a little bit before my time. But *The Beverly Hillbillies*: Now, *that* is quality TV. I was first aware of its artistic hold on me when I was 10, in 1966, and sat down to write my first novel. I soon recognized that I was (re)writing the pilot episode for the series, and thus my writing career never took off. I continue to be amused by cultural dislocations where the 'strange' visitors bring a fresh, funny, far-fetched but plausible interpretation to so-called modern life. In the case of the Clampets, it added to the appeal that they debunked the status symbols of jaded American aristocracy as slightly less convenient versions of the utilitarian fixtures of life in the Ozarks; the swimming pool became the cement pond. I liked the slightly irreverent and subversive class-war subtext in which the uneducated, unsophisticated hicks came across as sympathetic and wise, while the hoity-toity crowd were the buffoons. *The Marriage of Figaro* has a similar appeal, I suppose. My music similarly combines elements of so-called high and low culture. I see my own background as a natural precursor to that view: I was a lower-middle class kid who went to public school, worked summer jobs picking plums and peaches, and went on to a higher education that would have been available only to an aristocratic class less than one hundred years ago."

While pursuing that higher education at the University of California at Davis, Mackey decided, just out of curiosity, to sign up for an introductory music course taught by

Steven Mackey

(b. Frankfurt, Germany, February 14 1956)

He was born in Germany because his father was in the civil service, but he grew up in Marysville, California. He was already playing rock guitar when he enrolled as a physics major at the University of California at Davis, where an introductory course in music prompted him to change majors. It was only then that he learned to read music. He studied theory and composition with Andrew Frank, Richard Swift, and William Valente. He taught and played in a country and western band. He continued his education at the State University of New York at Stony Brook and at Brandeis, where he earned his doctorate. Today he teaches composition at Princeton. His many commissions have come from such sources as the San Francisco Symphony (*Lost & Found*, 1996, and *Pedal Tones*, 2002), the Chicago Symphony Orchestra (*Eating Greens*, 1994), and the New World Symphony, with which he performed as soloist in the world premiere of his electric-guitar concerto *Tuck and Roll* (2000) shortly before introducing the work to San Francisco in the American Mavericks festival.

Steven Mackey as soloist with the New World Symphony in his *Tuck and Roll.*

San Francisco Bay Area pianist Marvin Tartak. "That was my first contact with classical music, when I heard Stravinsky ballets and Mozart piano concertos for the first time, and I couldn't believe what I was hearing. Composer: No one had ever read me that job description before. I knew three professions: rock star, doctor, lawyer. Well, maybe nuclear physicist." He went to see Andrew Frank, one of the composers on the UC Davis faculty, about switching his major. Frank suggested he come in and take a test on guitar, the only instrument Mackey played: "We'll have you do some sight-reading." Mackey explained that, while he had "plenty of fingers," he did not read music. "Give it up," was Frank's advice, something about which he and Mackey still laugh.

Mackey did not give it up. Six years later, after he finished college, he knew more or less where his life was going. But the combination of teaching guitar by day, playing in a country and western band at night, and composing whenever he could did not work well. "The band made my ears ring. The dream seemed flawed." He learned to play the lute, turned "from a heavy-metal guitarist to a whole-wheat early-music lutenist," and for a time even imagined a future as director of an early-music consort.

Mackey has taught at Princeton now for more than a decade. For many years, Princeton, with Roger Sessions and Milton Babbitt on its faculty, was known as the head-quarters of what on Brahms's honorary degree citation from the University of Breslau is referred to as *ars musicae severioris.* Nowadays, Princeton is more diversified. It has professors who represent that distinguished "old guard" and those who work with computers and with found sonorous objects; its students run the gamut from those who do performance art to those who still compose on paper. Mackey himself composes on paper, which puts him at least some way toward the conservative end of the spectrum, and he points out that when (for example) he has written for amplified piano, as in his *a matter of life and death*, it is "at an exceedingly low level of technological sophistication."

Mackey's compositional approach continually harkens back to the high/low culture clash.

> *In my guitar concerto,* Tuck and Roll, *the electric guitar—merchandise available at Sears—is the hero/protagonist that guides instruments of greater economic value and far richer cultural traditions through a complicated musical landscape. At a certain point in the last movement, a mysterious cloud of string harmony recedes to reveal a solo chorus of cheap marine band harmonicas—the most "down-home" instrument I could think of. There are also many places in all of my music in which "old-world" instruments are asked to drop their refined veneers and squeak and squawk like household utensils. I'm not trying to make anyone the buffoon, but rather find a place that can accommodate a wide range of expression.*
>
> *In terms of my stylistic direction, I'm noticing my music change in ways that seem like predictable responses to age and, I hope, maturity. Ten years ago my music careened from extreme idea to extreme idea like a freestyle skier. I aspired to be blazingly inventive with an emphasis on precarious textures. As in my tennis game, I can't rely on my quickness any longer, and I have to make every move count more. So while the sense of motion and the rate of change is similar, the degree of change is reined in a little and hovers closer to a thematic core.*

Riley, Reich, Adams, Del Tredici, Monk, Zappa, Mackey: Theirs are mixed voices indeed, and they offer a mixed bag of styles, genres, techniques, experiences, attitudes, and, arguably, results. The scene they inhabit at the beginning of the 21st century can perhaps be characterized best as a culmination of the freedom that mavericks had been working toward for 100 years. As Adams has observed, "I and many composers of my generation feel ourselves living in a post-stylistic era. Maybe I was the first post-stylist." Certainly the lack of a powerful status quo has freed members of this generation to follow their urges. Whereas the willingness to employ dissonance once divided the musical adventurers from the cowards, no such clear indicator existed at the end of the 20th century to separate those who just wrote music from the mavericks.

postscript

Music for an Evolving World

BY MICHAEL TILSON THOMAS

The American Mavericks festival was an occasion to re-experience the range and depth of some of the originally inventive and iconoclastic works that perhaps best witness the profound and zany diversity of the United States. The festival was an outgrowth of an insatiable musical curiosity that has been with me since childhood. Indeed, many of these composers—such as Ives, Ruggles, Cage, and Harrison—I first encountered and performed in my teens. Though these composers now seem to me like old musical friends, I can still remember how perplexing, provocative, and even amusing they seemed to me when I first heard them. But a new piece, or a new composer with a fresh or startling perspective, has always evoked in me a desire to explore as a voyager who views an uncharted island for the first time. Frequently, I am cast in the triple role of explorer, performer, and partisan since new music needs persuasive performances in order to win over receptive listeners. We all come to the concert hall with certain expectations, and it is exciting to find these expectations challenged and changed—when that happens, there is always a certain amount of risk on both sides of the footlights.

In 1971, when I introduced Steve Reich's *Four Organs* at Carnegie Hall, the music caused a near-riot. Factions in the audience nearly came to blows. I guess you could call the performance both persuasive and risky. That evening, the audience's expectations were certainly challenged. Overnight, the shock waves of this concert hit the music world; and across the whole country, Steve's music and minimalism were suddenly much more known and discussed.

The experience of encountering the new is an essential part of being an audience member. So many different new ideas are set before the public in every new musical generation. The 20th century in particular presented more musical "isms" than any other in history. Audience members had to confront primitivism, serialism, neoclassicism, and minimalism— to name only a few—and come to grips with the musical message of each of these styles. Behind each was a whole world view—one shaped very much by the personality of the composers, but also by political and social events taking place in their countries and in the whole world. Increasingly, music has given voice to the feelings of dissatisfaction, defiance, and unease experienced by so many artists in our time. And concert music has grown ever closer to vernacular music. In earlier times, composers went to great lengths to "correct" the meandering or bizarre turns of folk music or other popular forms. But in our day, influenced by the power of recorded music, we've come to revel in the curious, rough-hewn musical qualities that untutored but fiercely intuitive performers have brought to our attention. So many of the maverick composers turned for their inspiration to music that was once considered outside the realm of the classically

June 2000: In conversation after a concert in the American Mavericks festival. From left: Meredith Monk, Lou Harrison, Michael Tilson Thomas, Lukas Foss.

correct, and they have tried to use that "other" music's unconscious power as a driving force for works in larger forms, for larger ensembles. How well they succeed in achieving this mix is something that can only be determined by time and by the audience. The audience has the responsibility of deciding, long after the shock of the premiere performance and long after the details of the program notes have been forgotten, whether or not the piece itself has enough to say so that it will stand on its own merits. The standard repertory contains many works that were at one time considered revolutionary, and the process through which they have become an essential part of our musical lives is one in which composers, performers, and audience members have a vital role.

The American maverick composers of the 20th century may have been the first composers really to grasp the world's continual evolution. Certainly the world was changing more rapidly than it had ever changed before, but these composers were the ones who sensed how to translate that change into art. They knew their music wouldn't necessarily be pretty, and they knew it would be unfamiliar to listeners because it reflected the life they saw, with which *no one* was familiar—a society in transition from farm to city, a world struggling in the aftermath of global war, a country reveling in the prosperity of the Jazz Age and plunged almost overnight into the throes of a Great Depression. And while they sought to give voice to this new world, they confirmed the intensity of being alive: in their pure unbridled creative exuberance, their search for new ways of making sounds, their willingness to pile ingredients into the blender, set the speed on high, and see what happened. They wanted to give voice to what they thought were rawer, truer, more fundamental relationships between people and music. What they composed wasn't "nice"—Charles Ives's favorite word to describe the kind of music that is merely decorative and refuses to get entangled in a world where alienation and injustice are as constant as sweetness and light. The San Francisco Symphony's American Mavericks festival in June 2000 focused on composers who weren't afraid of rolling up their sleeves and making music out of all the raw materials that their society presented them. They wrote what they had to write. They knew they weren't guaranteed performances. Some of them heard very little of their music and never knew if it would be played.

Those of us who make music in San Francisco are blessed with an audience that comes to the concert hall more to discover the world than to escape it. The mavericks should have been so lucky in their day. It has given me great satisfaction to play this music for listeners intent on new ways of hearing. And the evenings shared with Lou Harrison, Lukas Foss, Earle Brown, Steve Reich, David Del Tredici, John Adams, Meredith Monk, and Steve Mackey—in performances of their works and in discussion and consideration of earlier American music pioneers—have been some of the most exciting of my life.

Today, the maverick music of the 20th century is part of Western music's great tradition. We hear Mozart and Beethoven and Brahms differently because of the mavericks, and our vision is more complete because of them all. The mavericks help the world catch up to the present. Those of us who love music are lucky indeed to know the work of composers with the genius, the perceptiveness, the guts, the sheer nuts-and-bolts ability, and the desire to help us understand where we are in relation to the moment, and where we hope to be.

American Mavericks at the San Francisco Symphony: The Programs

Meet the Mavericks

MICHAEL TILSON THOMAS conducting

IVES *Quarter-tone Piano Piece* No. 2 (Alan Feinberg and Julie Steinberg, pianos)

CAGE *Credo in Us* for Piano, Percussion and Radio (Raymond Froehlich and Jack Van Geem, percussion; Alan Feinberg and Peter Grunberg, pianos)

FELDMAN *Piece for 4 Pianos* (Michael Tilson Thomas, Alan Feinberg, Peter Grunberg, and Michael Linville, pianos)

BABBITT *Philomel* for Soprano and Tape (Lauren Flanigan, soprano)

RILEY *In C* (members of the San Francisco Symphony and members of the audience)

Maverick Icons

MICHAEL TILSON THOMAS conducting

RUGGLES *Sun-treader*

CRAWFORD SEEGER Andante for Strings (from String Quartet)

FOSS *Time Cycle* (Lauren Flanigan, soprano)

MONK Four *a cappella* pieces from the opera *ATLAS* (Meredith Monk and Vocal Ensemble, with members of the San Francisco Symphony Chorus)

IVES Symphony No. 4 (with the San Francisco Symphony Chorus; Michael Linville, piano; Alexander Frey, organ)

A Tribute to Duke Ellington

JON FADDIS conducting
QUEEN ESTHER MARROW vocalist
PRISCILLA BASKERVILLE soprano
MILT GRAYSON vocalist
SAN FRANCISCO SYMPHONY CHORUS

Harlem
New World a-Comin' (Renée Rosnes, piano)
Take the "A" Train
(In My) Solitude
I'm Beginning to See the Light

From the Sacred Concerts:
In the Beginning God
Tell Me it's the Truth
Heaven
David Danced

The Lord's Prayer
The Shepherd
Freedom
Come Sunday
My Love
Praise God and Dance

JUNE 11, 2000

The World of George Antheil

MICHAEL TILSON THOMAS conducting

Sonata No. 2 for Violin with Piano and Drums (Abel-Steinberg-Winant Trio)
A Jazz Symphony (Michael Linville, piano; Mark Inouye, trumpet)
Ballet mécanique

JUNE 15, 2000

A Tribute to Lou Harrison

MICHAEL TILSON THOMAS conducting

Symphony No. 3
Suite for Violin with American Gamelan (Chee-Yun, violin, with San Francisco Symphony percussionists)
Concerto for Organ with Percussion Orchestra (John Walker, organ)

JUNE 16, 2000

America Underground

MICHAEL TILSON THOMAS conducting

(Pre-concert recital with pianist Ursula Oppens performing Elliott Carter's *Two Diversions*, *Retrouvailles*, and *90+*)

CAGE *Dance/4 Orchestras* (Michael Tilson Thomas, Alasdair Neale, Peter Grunberg, Apo Hsu, conductors)

COWELL Piano Concerto (Ursula Oppens, piano)

DEL TREDICI *Adventures Underground* (Lauren Flanigan, soprano)

VARÈSE *Amériques*

JUNE 17 AND 18, 2000

Steve Reich and Musicians

REICH *Music for 18 Musicians*

REICH/KOROT *Three Tales*, A Documentary Video Opera. Act I: *Hindenburg* (Steve Reich and Musicians, Synergy)

JUNE 20, 2000

From Ives to Electricity

MICHAEL TILSON THOMAS conducting the New World Symphony

BROWN *Cross Sections and Color Fields*

MACKEY *Tuck and Roll* for Electric Guitar and Orchestra (Steve Mackey, guitar)

IVES Symphony No. 2

JUNE 21, 2000

American Mavericks, A to Z

JOHN ADAMS conducting the New World Symphony

ZAPPA *Dupree's Paradise*

ADAMS *Shaker Loops*

NANCARROW Study No. 6 (arr. Mikhashoff):

ADAMS *Grand Pianola Music* (Gideon Rubin and Michael Linville, pianos; Olive Simpson, Micaela Haslam, and Heather Cairncross, vocalists)

JUNE 23 AND 24, 2000

A Copland Journey

MICHAEL TILSON THOMAS conducting

The Cat and the Mouse (Peter Grunberg, piano)
Prologue from *Music for the Theatre*
Piano Variations (Michael Tilson Thomas, piano)
El Salón México
In the Beginning (Bridgett Hooks, soprano, and San Francisco Symphony Chorus)
Danzón Cubano
The Golden Willow Tree, from *Old American Songs* (San Francisco Symphony Chorus)
Inscape
The Chariot, from *Twelve Poems of Emily Dickinson* (Bridgett Hooks, soprano; Peter Grunberg, piano)
Finale from Third Symphony

Notes

CHAPTER ONE The American Maverick Tradition

Page 2. "Music was born free," from "Sketch for a New Aesthetic of Music" reprinted in *Contemporary Composers on Contemporary Music* (Da Capo, 1998), 3-16.

CHAPTER TWO The Maverick and the Public

Page 11. "Prologue to the Annual Tragedy," Paul Rosenfeld, *Musical Chronicle* (1917-1923) (New York: Harcourt, Brace and Company, 1923), 3-10. The piece was written in August 1921 and originally published without the title in Rosenfeld's "Musical Chronicle" column in *The Dial 71* (1921), 487-491.

CHAPTER THREE Search for the Modern: Early 20th-Century Mavericks

Page 19. "A composer who has not the slightest idea of self-ridicule." Olin Downes on Ives is cited in Ian Crofton and Donald Fraser's, *A Dictionary of Musical Quotations* (New York: Schirmer, 1985), 83; that book cites in turn the *New York Times*, 1927. In his *Charles Ives: A Life in Music* (New York: Norton, 1996, 368), Jan Swafford provides a longer citation from that source, given as *New York Times*, January 30, 1927, from which context we see that it was actually meant as a sort of compliment, not implied by the Crofton/Fraser context. The article was written after hearing the two movements of the Fourth Symphony, and Downes finds it is endowed with "a 'gumption,' as the New Englander would say, not derived from some 'Sacre de printemps,' or from anything but the conviction of a composer who has not the slightest idea of self-ridicule and who dares to jump with feet and hands and a reckless somersault or two on his way."

"Peter Burkholder has remarked..." Burkholder's major analytical work on Ives and his vernacular sources is *All Made of Tunes: Charles Ives and the Uses of Musical Borrowing* (New Haven: Yale University Press, 1995).

Page 21. Harrison's remarks were made in a post-concert discussion in the American Mavericks festival, June 9, 2000.

Page 22. "There is not much to say...." Ives's comments on his Second Symphony are quoted in liner notes by George K. Diehl (BMG High Performance 09026-63316-2, 1973).

Page 24. "Henry Cowell summed him up." Cowell's description of Ruggles is from Lou Harrison's *About Carl Ruggles* (New York: Oscar Baradinsky, 1946).

"The eclecticism of Ives's technique..." Wilfred Mellers, *Music in a New Found Land* (Stonehill Publishing Co., 1975), 66.

Page 26. "...the future which Varèse sees with the intensity of a prophet..." *Santa Fe New Mexican* August 21, 1936, 2.

Page 28. "Our new medium has brought to composers..." Reprinted in *Contemporary Composers on Contemporary Music*, 207-208.

"There is no avant-garde: only some people a bit behind." Varèse is quoted in *Chambers Music Quotations*, compiled by Derek Watson (Edinburgh: W & R Chamber, 1991), 99.

Varèse "fathered forth noise into 20th-century music." "History of Experimental Music in the United States" (1958), reprinted in *Silence*, 69.

"Virgil Thomson noted that 'the variety of [Henry Cowell's] sources and composing methods is probably the broadest of our time." Virgil Thomson, *American Music Since 1910* (New York: Holt, Rinhart and Winston, 1972), 135.

Page 32. Gann on Henry Cowell from *The Whole World of Music: A Henry Cowell Symposium*, ed. David Nicholls (Harwood Academic Press, 1997), 221-222.

Page 33. "A good dissonance is like a man." For a historical survey of this and other misogynistic rhetoric in the early 20th century, see Catherine Parsons Smith, "'A Distinguishing Virility': Feminism and Modernism in

American Art Music," in *Cecilia Reclaimed: Feminist Perspectives on Gender and Music*, ed. Susan C. Cook and Judy S. Tsou (University of Illinois Press, 1994), 90-106.

"Carl Ruggles swears in every sentence...." Quoted in Judith Tick, *Ruth Crawford Seeger: A Composer's Search for American Music* (Oxford University Press, 1997), 111.

Page 34. "Accumulating tension like a spring..." Tick, 215.

"spirit of me/Dear rollicking far-gazing straddler of two worlds." Quoted in Tick, 96.

CHAPTER FOUR Finding an American Sound: Two Contemporaries

Page 39. "I was spoiled rotten." Edward Kennedy Ellington, *Music is My Mistress* (Da Capo, 1976; orig. pub. 1973), 6.

Page 41. "I try to catch the character and mood and feeling of my people." Grover Sales recalls the source of this quotation as the 1931 press book produced by Ellington's manager, Irving Mills.

Page 42. "Governor! You've got to pay me more money!" quoted by Gus Matzorkis in liner notes to Ben Webster recordings in *Giants of Jazz* (Time-Life), 20.

"If he had been born white..." The commentator was Grover Sales, who worked with Ellington as a publicist.

Page 44. "Fate is being kind to me." *Music is My Mistress*, 286.

"We look to the future for the American composer." Quoted in Rudi Blesh and Harriet Janis, *They All Played Ragtime* (Oak Publications), 134.

Page 45. "There was a lot of fun in bucking the tide." Aaron Copland and Vivian Perlis, *Copland 1900-1942* (New York: St. Martin's/Marek, 1984), 123.

"I was anxious to write a work that would immediately be recognized as American." Aaron Copland, "Composer from Brooklyn: An Autobiographical Sketch," originally published in 1939 in the *Magazine of Art*, slightly revised and reprinted in Aaron Copland, *The New Music, 1900-1960* (New York: Norton, 1968), 158.

Page 46. "If a young man at the age of twenty-three can write a symphony like that, in five years he will be ready to commit murder." Walter Damrosch is quoted in Aaron Copland, "Composer from Brooklyn," 157.

"In those days, it was clear that you had to be 'finished' in Europe. You couldn't be 'finished' in America." Edward T. Cone, "Conversation with Aaron Copland," in Benjamin Boretz and Edward T. Cone (eds.), *Perspectives on American Composers* (New York: Norton, 1971), 133.

"The conviction grew inside me..." Aaron Copland, *Music and Imagination* (Harvard University Press, 1952), 99.

Page 47. Jerome D. Bohm wrote in the *Herald Tribune*: "Mr. Copland, always a composer of radical tendencies, has in these variations sardonically thumbed his nose at all of those esthetic attributes which have hitherto been considered essential to the creation of music.'" *Copland 1900-1942*, 179. "...after a 1958 performance of the orchestral version of the piece, Howard Taubman wrote in the *Times*..." Taubman, in a review of a December 5, 1958 performance by Leonard Bernstein and the New York Philharmonic, is quoted in *Copland 1900-1942*, 184.

Page 48. "It does not incorporate folk music or jazz materials." Aaron Copland and Vivian Perlis: *Copland Since 1943* (New York: St. Martin's Press, 1989), 73.

"I was interested in the simple outlines of the theory." Comments by Copland quoted in the liner notes for the recording of *Connotations* by Leonard Bernstein and the New York Philharmonic (Columbia MS7431).

Page 49. "...keeping the faith..." Milton Babbitt in conversation with Michael Steinberg at a new-music concert in the late 1950s at Martha Graham's studio, New York. The fact that the performance had received little publicity and was low-profile did not keep Copland from attending.

"It was a Copland talent...." *Copland Since 1943*, 420.

CHAPTER FIVE New Sources of Musical Sound: Technology and the Junkyard

Page 53. "anti-expressive, anti-romantic coldly mechanistic aesthetic..." George Antheil, *Bad Boy of Music*, (Samuel French, 1990; orig. pub. 1945), 8.

"Quel précision!" *Bad Boy of Music*, 133.

Page 58. "...one of the most significant artistic events of the 1920s..." Sylvia Beach, *Shakespeare & Company* (Harcourt, Brace, 1959), 124. The actual quote is "one of the big events of the twenties."

"People began to call each other names...." Bravig Imbs, "Confessions of Another Young Man" (Henkle-Yewdale, 1936), 100-102.

"outsacking the *Sacre*." Aaron Copland in a letter to Israel Citkowitz, quoted in Copland and Perlis, *Copland 1900-1942*, 127.

"From this moment on I knew that..." *Bad Boy of Music*, 134

Page 59. "...trying to make a mountain out of an Antheil." *New York Herald Tribune*, April 11, 1927.

"Some of the rhythms developed through the present acoustical investigation." Cowell, *New Musical Resources*, (Something Else Press, Inc., 1969), 64-65.

Page 62. "The measure of his achievement..." Kyle Gann, *The Music of Conlon Nancarrow* (Cambridge University Press, 1995), 35.

Page 64. "He was very open, and he took *you* seriously." Lou Harrison in conversation with Michael Steinberg, August 1995.

Page 68. "[Fischinger] made a remark to me which dropped me into the world of noise." Quoted in William Duckworth, "Anything I Say Will Be Misunderstood: An Interview with John Cage," in *John Cage at Seventy-Five*, special issue of *Bucknell Review* (Associated University Presses, 1989), 18-19.

"Schoenberg said I would never be able to compose." John Cage, reporting on Schoenberg's assessment of his potential as a composer, is cited in Crofton and Fraser's *A Dictionary of Musical Quotations*, 28.

CHAPTER SIX Control and Beyond: The Postwar Avant-Garde

Page 73. "...simply a way to wake up to the very life we're living." "Experimental Music" in John Cage, *Silence: Lectures and Writings* (Wesleyan University Press, 1961), 12.

Page 74. "It is to prepare you for daily life." John Cage in a lecture at a new-music festival at the State University of New York, Buffalo, ca. 1966-67.

"His freshness came from an absence of knowledge." Quoted in Joan Peyser, *Boulez* (Schirmer, 1976), 85.

Page 75. "How one reacts to Cage's ideas seems to me..." Aaron Copland, *The New Music, 1900-1960* (New York: Norton, 1968), 178.

Page 76. "The main influence from Cage..." This and the other quotes from Feldman are from "I Met Heine on the Rue Fürstenburg," *Buffalo Evening News*, April 21, 1973.

Page 78. "My whole generation was hung up on the 20 to 25 minute piece." Feldman is quoted in an undated brochure on his music, published by Universal Edition.

Page 79. "There is no final solution to this paradox...." Quoted in Michael Nyman, "Inauguration 1950-60: Feldman, Brown, Wolff, Cage" in Richard Kostelanetz and Joseph Darby, eds., *Classic Essays on Twentieth-Century Music: A Continuing Symposium* (Schirmer, 1996), 189.

Page 80. Earle Brown's reflections are from correspondence with Susan Key, spring 2000 and 2001.

Page 84. "Who Cares If You Listen" is reprinted in *Contemporary Composers on Contemporary Music*, 243-250.

"Performance practice is for mediocrities." Lukas Foss in conversation with Michael Steinberg, San Francisco, October 1984. Foss was in town to conduct the San Francisco Symphony in a series of un-historically informed performances of J.S. Bach's *Brandenburg* Concertos.

Page 87. Foss's remarks were made at a post-concert discussion in the American Mavericks festival, June 9, 2000.

CHAPTER SEVEN Mixed Voices: The '60s Generation

Page 91. "...as much a watershed as Stravinsky's *Rite of Spring*..." Ed Ward, *The Wall Street Journal,* February 12, 1997.

Page 97. "A *Time* magazine article in 1982..." Michael Walsh, "The Heart is Back in the Game," *Time,* September 20, 1982.

"*Shaker Loops* began as a string quartet...." Adams's comments are from program notes he prepared for the San Francisco Symphony performance of June 21, 2000.

Page 98. "I was thunderstruck by the simplicity and power of the emotions," quoted in Alex Ross, "The Harmonist," *The New Yorker,* January 8, 2001, 43.

"...driving across the Bay Bridge..." Interview with Jonathan Cott, liner notes for recording of *Harmonielehre* (Nonesuch P 79115).

Page 102. "I don't try to turn my back aggressively on the past...." Interview with Michael Steinberg, February 1985.

Page 104. "With nonsense I felt somehow I could do whatever I wanted...." Del Tredici is quoted in Richard Dufallo's *Trackings* (New York: Oxford, 1989), 161.

Page 105. "Overt tonal proclamations, fanfares, and pretty tunes..." "David Del Tredici," in Nicolas Slonimsky, *Baker's Biographical Dictionary of Musicians* (New York: Schirmer Books, 1992).

Page 106. "My latest creative impulse is toward wholeness." Comments on *Gay Life*, in James M. Keller's program note on that work, San Francisco Symphony program book, May 3-5, 2001.

Page 109. "I've always thought of the voice as a language itself." *Talking Music: Conversations with John Cage, Philip Glass, Laurie Anderson and Five Generations of American Experimental Composers*, ed. William Duckworth (Da Capo Press, 1995), 359.

Page 115. Steven Mackey: Correspondence with Susan Key, fall 2001.

"I and many composers of my generation..." John Adams, talk at the San Francisco Performing Arts Library and Museum, November 14, 2000.

Comments by San Francisco Symphony musicians and guest artists are from interviews and correspondence with Susan Key between December 2000 and April 2001. Comments by Michael Tilson Thomas were delivered from the stage during the American Mavericks festival.

Illustration Credits

We gratefully acknowledge the following individuals and institutions for the use of the visual materials in these pages (photographers' names are in italics):

Christine Alcino: 99

Estate of George Antheil: 53, 56, 57, 58

Alice Arnold: 113

Earle Brown: 79

Boosey & Hawkes: 104

Stefan Cohen: 32

Betty Freeman: 60, 61, 69, 73, 77, 81, 83, 93

Greg Gorman: 111

Jim Hair: 63

Collection of Lou Harrison: 62, 64, 66, 67

David Harsany: 65

Robin Holland: 105

Don Hunstein: 23, 25

Family of Bruce Kueffer: 4

Kristen Loken: 102, 106, 118

Man Ray Trust/Artists Rights Society: 26

Collection of Olivia Mattis: 26

Terrence McCarthy: 55, 94, 114

Joel Meyerowitz: 95

Meredith Monk: 108

Musical America Archives: 5, 12, 14, 27, 31, 45, 100

C.F. Peters: 76

F.W. Olin Library, Mills College: 68

Rutgers Institute of Jazz Studies Archives: 39, 40, 41, 43

San Francisco Performing Arts Library and Museum: 46

San Francisco Public Library: 5, 12, 14, 29, 74, 100

F. Scott Schafer: 107

G. Schirmer: 30 (Piano Concerto by Henry Cowell. Copyright ©1930 by Editions Maurice Senart. International Copyright Secured. All Rights Reserved. Reprinted by Permission of Editions Salabert and G. Schirmer, Inc.—ASCAP)

Mike Seeger: 33, 35

Collection of Michael Tilson Thomas: 47, 49

Collection of Judith Tick: 33, 35

Universal Editions: outside back cover, 80

Yale University Library: 21, 24

Tom Zimberoff: ix, 85, 86

A Selective Bibliography, and a Highly Selective Discography

BY ALAN RICH

GENERAL SURVEYS

Two classic surveys of American music, with particular regard for the Maverick spirit, are currently out of print: Wilfred Mellers's *Music in a New Found Land* and John Rockwell's *All-American Music*. The maverick element in American music has attracted several writers in the past decade. Carol Oja has been particularly drawn to the "formative" years of the 1920s. My *American Pioneers* deals with the impact of Ives, Varèse, Cowell, and Cage, and comes up to date with such figures as Earle Brown. It is included in Phaidon Press's vast 20th-Century Composers series, as is K. Robert Schwarz's survey of the minimalists. The following bibliography leans toward composers identifiable as "mavericks." For a more rounded (if slightly outdated) overview of American music, the four-volume *New Grove Dictionary of American Music*, published in 1986 by Macmillan, maintains its authority.

Broyles, Michael. *Mavericks and Other Traditions in American Music* (Yale University Press, forthcoming)

Crawford, Richard. *America's Musical Life: A History* (W.W. Norton, 2001)

Duckworth, William. *Talking Music: Conversations with John Cage, Philip Glass, Laurie Anderson and Five Generations of American Experimental Composers* (Da Capo Press, 1995).

Gann, Kyle. *American Music in the Twentieth Century* (Wadsworth/Thomson Learning, 1997)

Giddins, Gary. *Visions of Jazz: The First Century* (Oxford University Press, 1998)

Oja, Carol. *Making Music Modern: New York in the 1920s* (Oxford University Press, 1999)

Rich, Alan. *American Pioneers* (Phaidon Press, 1995)

Schaefer, John. *New Sounds, A Listener's Guide to New Music* (Harper, 1987)

Schwarz, K. Robert. *Minimalists* (Phaidon Press, 1996)

COMPOSERS

George Antheil

▶ Antheil, George. *Bad Boy of Music* (Samuel French, 1981)

John Cage

▶ Cage, John. *Silence: Lectures and Writings* (Wesleyan University Press, 1961)

▶ Kostelanetz, Richard (ed.). *John Cage, Writer* Selected texts and essays by Cage (Cooper Square Press, 1993)

▶ Duckworth, William and Fleming, Richard (co-eds.). *John Cage at 75: Collected Essays* (Bucknell University Press, 1989) Reading Cage's own writing is the best way to hear his music.

Aaron Copland

▶ Pollack, Howard. *Aaron Copland: The Life and Work of an Uncommon Man* (Henry Holt, 1999)

▶ Copland, Aaron and Perlis, Vivian. *Copland, 1900-1942* (St. Martin's/Marek, 1984)
Copland, Aaron and Perlis, Vivian. *Copland Since 1943* (St. Martin's Press, 1989)

Henry Cowell

▶ No extended biographical writings are currently available; several are announced as "in preparation."

▶ Cowell, Henry. *New Musical Resources*, with notes and an accompanying essay by David Nicholls (Cambridge University Press, 1996)

Ruth Crawford Seeger

▶ Tick, Judith. *Ruth Crawford Seeger, A Composer's Search for American Music* (Oxford University Press, 1997)

Duke Ellington

▶ Nicholson, Stuart. *Reminiscing in Tempo: A Portrait of Duke Ellington* (Northeastern University Press, 1999)

▶ Collier, James Lincoln. *Duke Ellington* (Oxford University Press, 1987) A controversial point of view about the relative merits of Ellington's popular standards versus his longer, more ambitious compositions.

Robert Erickson

▶ Shere, Charles. *Thinking Sound Music* (Fallen Leaf Press, 1995) Erickson, though virtually neglected today, was the great guiding spirit behind San Francisco's Tape Music Center. Contains a CD sampler of works by the composer.

Morton Feldman

▶ Friedman, B.H. (ed.). *"Give My Regards to Eighth Street": Collected Writings of Morton Feldman* (Exact Change Press, 2000)

Lou Harrison

▶ Miller, Leta E. and Lieberman, Fredric. *Lou Harrison, Composing a World* (Oxford University Press, 1998) Contains a CD sampler of works by the composer.

Charles Ives

▶ Swafford, Jan. *Charles Ives: A Life With Music* (Norton, 1996)

Harry Partch

▶ Partch, Harry. *Genesis of a Music* (University of Wisconsin Press, 1974)

Blackburn, Philip (ed.). *Enclosures iii* (American Composers Forum, 1997) A "scrapbook" of Harry Partch materials.

▶ Gilmore, Bob. *Harry Partch: A Biography* (Yale University Press, 1998)

Edgard Varèse

▶ Bernard, Jonathan W. *The Music of Edgard Varèse* (Yale University Press, 1987)

RECORDINGS

From the brash, exuberant William Henry Fry, who dared to compose an American symphony (inspired by Santa Claus!) in the 1850s, even before Sam Maverick emancipated his cattle, to the intensity of John Adams's *El Niño* 150 years later, the audible evidence of America's breakthrough spirit is glowing and intense. Never mind the famous John Cage dictum "take away the records, and people will learn to sing"; even Cage's notorious "silent" piece, *4'33"* makes its convincing case on disc. (It's "played" by Frank Zappa on a Koch two-disc set.) This selection is intended merely as foundation; be warned, furthermore, that since challenging contemporary music enjoys minimal popularity against, say, the tone poems of Richard Strauss, record companies remove slow-selling items on brutally short notice.

John Adams

▶ *Century Rolls* (Emanuel Ax, piano, Cleveland Orchestra/Christoph von Dohnányi), *Slonimsky's Earbox, Lollapalooza* (Hallé Orchestra/Kent Nagano) Nonesuch

▶ *El Niño* (Deutsches Symphonie Orchester Berlin, soloists and chorus/Kent Nagano) Nonesuch

▶ *Grand Pianola Music* (London Sinfonietta/John Adams) Nonesuch

▶ *Harmonielehre* (San Francisco Symphony/Edo de Waart) Nonesuch

▶ *Naïve and Sentimental Music* (Los Angeles Philharmonic/Esa Pekka Salonen) Nonesuch

George Antheil

▶ *Antheil Plays Antheil*—music from Antheil's later "neo-romantic" period, including recordings of Antheil at the piano and recordings of Antheil speaking. An Other Minds recording, available only through the Other Minds web site, http://otherminds.org/html/Antheilcd.html

▶ *Ballet mécanique, A Jazz Symphony*, short works (Ensemble Modern/H.K. Gruber) RCA

▶ *Ballet mécanique* and other works for player pianos, percussion, and electronics—world premiere recording of the sixteen-player-piano version of the *Ballet mécanique* (Electronic Music Foundation)

▶ *A Jazz Symphony*, included in the collection *New World Jazz*, with works by Milhaud, Gershwin, Stravinsky, Bernstein, and Adams (New World Symphony/Micheal Tilson Thomas) RCA

Milton Babbitt

▶ *Works for Piano* (Robert Taub) Harmonia Mundi

Earle Brown

▶ *Windsor Jambs, Tracking Pierrot, Centering* (San Francisco Contemporary Players/Stephen Mosko) Newport Classic

John Cage

▶ *A Chance Operation*—various short works including *4'33"* and *Living Room Music* (Various artists, including Frank Zappa) Koch

▶ *Sonatas and Interludes, Imaginary Landscape Retrospective Concert* (Various artists, including Cage) Wergo

▶ *Works for Percussion* (Hélios Quartet) Wergo

Aaron Copland

▶ *Copland the Modernist*—includes the *Piano Concerto* (with Garrick Ohlsson), *Orchestral Variations, Short Symphony* (San Francisco Symphony/Michael Tilson Thomas) RCA

▶ *Copland the Populist*—includes *Appalachian Spring, Billy the Kid, Rodeo* (San Francisco Symphony/Michael Tilson Thomas) RCA

▶ *Piano Music* (Stephen Hough) (Hyperion)

Henry Cowell

▶ *Piano Music* (Henry Cowell) Smithsonian

▶ *Quartet Euphometric* (Emerson Quartet) Deutsche Grammophon

Ruth Crawford Seeger

▶ *Quartet* (Arditti Quartet) Gramavision

▶ *Ruth Crawford Seeger: Portrait* Works by Ruth Crawford and Charles Seeger. Deutsche Grammophon

David Del Tredici

▶ *In Memory of a Summer Day* (Phyllis Bryn-Julson, St. Louis Symphony/Leonard Slatkin) Nonesuch

Duke Ellington

▶ *The Blanton-Webster Band*—a three-CD set with sixty-six songs representing Ellington's most fertile creative association. RCA

▶ *The Classic Ellington* (City of Birmingham Symphony Orchestra/Simon Rattle) A fascinating musical collaboration featuring top-notch performers in classical and jazz. EMI

Morton Feldman

▶ *Coptic Light* (New World Symphony/Michael Tilson Thomas) Argo

▶ *For Philip Guston* (California EAR Unit) Bridge

▶ *Rothko Chapel* (University of California Chorus/Philip Brett) New Albion

Lukas Foss

▶ *Time Cycle* (Adele Addison, New York Philharmonic/Leonard Bernstein) Sony

William Henry Fry

▶ *Santa Claus Symphony* (1853) (Scottish National Orchestra/Tony Rowe) Naxos

George Gershwin

▶ *Rhapsody in Blue, An American in Paris* (George Gershwin, from 1925 piano roll; Columbia Jazz Orchestra/Michael Tilson Thomas) Sony

Philip Glass

▶ *Einstein on the Beach* (Glass Ensemble/Michael Riesman) Nonesuch

▶ *Music in Twelve Parts* (Glass Ensemble) Nonesuch

▶ *Symphony No. 5* (various choruses, Ana Maria Martinez, Denyce Graves, Michael Schade, Eric Owens, Albert Dohmen, Vienna Radio Symphony/Dennis Russell Davies) Nonesuch

Lou Harrison

▶ *Harrison: A Portrait* (California Symphony/Barry Jekowsky) Includes *Symphony No. 4* and *Double Music* (collaboration with John Cage) Argo

▶ *La Koro Sutro*—includes the *Suite for Violin with American Gamelan* (University of California Chorus/Philip Brett) New Albion

▶ *Suite for Violin, Piano and Small Orchestra; Piano Concerto* (Keith Jarrett, New Japan Philharmonic/Naoto Otomo) New World

▶ *Symphony No. 3, Grand Duo for Violin and Piano* (Cabrillo Music Festival Orchestra/Dennis Russell Davies) BMG

▶ *Violin Concerto, Organ Concerto* (Shapiro, Craighead, Percussion Ensemble/William Kraft) Crystal

Charles Ives

▶ *Piano Sonata No. 2, Concord* (Gilbert Kalish) Nonesuch

▶ *A Symphony: New England Holidays, The Unanswered Question, Central Park in the Dark* (Chicago Symphony Orchestra/Michael Tilson Thomas) Sony

▶ *Symphonies Nos. 1 and 4* (Chicago Symphony Orchestra/Michael Tilson Thomas) Sony

▶ *Symphonies Nos. 2 and 3* (Royal Concertgebouw Orchestra/Michael Tilson Thomas) Sony

▶ *Three Places in New England, Central Park in the Dark* (Boston Symphony Orchestra/Michael Tilson Thomas) Deutsche Grammophon

Steven Mackey

▶ *Ravenshead*, Opera in Two Acts (Paul Dresher Ensemble) MinMax

▶ *Tuck and Roll* (Steven Mackey, New World Symphony/Michael Tilson Thomas) BMG

Meredith Monk

▶ *ATLAS, Opera in 3 Acts* (Houston Grand Opera/Meredith Monk) ECM

Conlon Nancarrow

▶ *Studies for Player Piano*, Volumes 1-5 (Conlon Nancarrow) Wergo

Horatio Parker

▶ *Hora Novissima* (1893) (Nebraska Wesleyan University Choir/John Levick) Albany

Harry Partch

▶ *Barstow: Eight Hitchhiker Inscriptions* (Ben Johnston, Kronos Quartet) Nonesuch

▶ *The Delusion of the Fury* (UCLA Ensemble) Innova

Steve Reich

▶ *The Desert Music* (Brooklyn Philharmonic Orchestra and Chorus, Michael Tilson Thomas) Nonesuch

▶ *Different Trains* (Kronos Quartet) Nonesuch

▶ *Music for 18 Musicians* (Steve Reich and Musicians) Nonesuch

Terry Riley

▶ *In C* (Terry Riley and friends) New Albion

▶ *Piano Music* (Terry Riley) New Albion

Carl Ruggles

▶ *Sun-treader, Men and Mountains* (Cleveland Orchestra/Christoph von Dohnányi) Philips

▶ *Sun-treader*—includes Walter Piston's *Symphony No. 2* (Boston Symphony Orchestra/ Michael Tilson Thomas) Deutsche Grammophon

Edgard Varèse

▶ *Ionisation, Amériques, Arcana, Density 21.5, Intégrales* (New York Philharmonic/Pierre Boulez) Sony

▶ *Amériques, Arcana, Ionisation, Déserts* (Chicago Symphony Orchestra/Pierre Boulez) Deutsche Grammophon

Frank Zappa

▶ *The Perfect Stranger, Girl in the Magnesium Dress*, other works (Paris Ensemble/Pierre Boulez) Ryko

▶ *Strictly Genteel, Bob in Dacron, Bogus Pomp*, etc. (London Symphony Orchestra/Kent Nagano) Ryko

Contributors

Paul Attinello, a specialist in avant-garde music of the 1960s, taught for many years at the University of Hong Kong.

William (Bill) Bennett joined the San Francisco Symphony in 1979 and is now Principal Oboist. He has been a soloist with the Orchestra on numerous occasions and in 1992 gave the world premiere of John Harbison's Oboe Concerto, a work written for him, and which he recorded with the Orchestra for London Records.

Michael Broyles is Distinguished Professor of Music and Professor of American History at The Pennsylvania State University. His book *Mavericks and Other Traditions in American Music* is forthcoming from Yale University Press. With Denise Von Glahn he is also writing a biography of Leo Ornstein. His most recent book is *"Music of the Highest Class": Elitism and Populism in Antebellum Boston.*

James M. Keller, the San Francisco Symphony's program annotator, is winner of the 1999 Deems Taylor Award for Music Journalism and is also program annotator for the New York Philharmonic.

Susan Key (editor), a musicologist specializing in American music, has taught at the University of Maryland, the College of William and Mary, and Stanford University. She is currently a member of the San Francisco Symphony's Artistic Planning Department.

Paul D. Lehrman is a composer, writer, and music technologist currently on the faculty of Tufts University. He has written scores for films featured on PBS, The History Channel, and Discovery networks, and he is co-author of *MIDI for the Professional* (AMSCO) and editorial director for the web site of the professional audio journal *Mix,* for which he writes a monthly column.

Alan Rich is the author of *American Pioneers* in Phaidon Press's 20th-Century Composers series. One of the founders of the San Francisco Bay Area station KPFA-FM, he moved on to become chief music critic for the *New York Herald Tribune* and *New York* magazine. He is currently classical music critic for the *LA Weekly.*

Larry Rothe (editor) has been editor of the San Francisco Symphony's program book since 1984. His articles have appeared in *Playbill*, *Stagebill*, and *Symphony* magazines, and he has contributed program notes and essays to the New York Philharmonic and Boston Symphony.

Grover Sales began working with Duke Ellington in the 1940s as writer and publicist. He is currently lecturer in Jazz Studies at Stanford University, the San Francisco Conservatory of Music, and the Jazz School in Berkeley. His book *Jazz: America's Classical Music* is used as a basic text in colleges nationwide.

K. Robert Schwarz was an American freelance music journalist who contributed regularly to the *New York Times*, *Classic CD*, *Out*, *Opera News*, and other publications. His articles on minimalism appeared in *Perspectives of New Music* and *American Music*, and he authored the volume *Minimalism* in Phaidon Press's 20th-Century Composers series.

Michael Steinberg served as program annotator for the San Francisco Symphony for twenty years and is currently a contributing writer to its program book. He has also been program annotator for the New York Philharmonic and Boston Symphony, and he is the former music critic of the *Boston Globe*. Two collections of his program essays, *The Symphony: A Listener's Guide* and *The Concerto: A Listener's Guide* have been published by Oxford University Press.

Michael Tilson Thomas, Music Director of the San Francisco Symphony since 1995, is also founder and Artistic Director of the New World Symphony. He has served as Principal Conductor of the London Symphony Orchestra and is now its Principal Guest Conductor, and he has been Music Director of the Buffalo Philharmonic and held major conducting appointments with the Los Angeles Philharmonic and Boston Symphony Orchestra. *Viva Voce*, his volume of conversations with critic Edward Seckerson, is published by Faber. His own compositions have been performed around the world.

Index

AMERICAN MAVERICKS

LIST OF CD CONTENTS

1 CHARLES IVES *Quarter-tone Piano Piece No. 2,* Allegro 3:48

2 MICHAEL TILSON THOMAS AND LOU HARRISON in conversation, June 9, 2000 1:08

3 HENRY COWELL Opening of Piano Concerto 3:01

4 GEORGE ANTHEIL Opening of *Ballet mécanique* 2:55

5 LOU HARRISON introducing his Concerto for Organ with Percussion Orchestra 1:48

6 LOU HARRISON Allegro from Concerto for Organ with Percussion Orchestra 3:04

7 MICHAEL TILSON THOMAS introducing Cage's *Credo in Us* 3:28

8 JOHN CAGE *Credo in Us* 12:22

9 MICHAEL TILSON THOMAS introducing Feldman's *Piece for 4 Pianos* 3:23

10 MORTON FELDMAN *Piece for 4 Pianos* 11:19

11 MICHAEL TILSON THOMAS AND LUKAS FOSS in conversation, June 9, 2000 1:02

12 MICHAEL TILSON THOMAS AND LUKAS FOSS in conversation, June 9, 2000 :32

13 MICHAEL TILSON THOMAS AND JOHN ADAMS in conversation, June 21, 2000 3:23

14 MICHAEL TILSON THOMAS AND DAVID DEL TREDICI in conversation, June 16, 2000 3:09

15 DAVID DEL TREDICI Opening of *Adventures Underground* 3:03

16 MEREDITH MONK on her stylistic development, June 9, 2000 1:23

17 MICHAEL TILSON THOMAS AND STEVE MACKEY in conversation, June 20, 2000 3:16

18 STEVE MACKEY "Intrigue" from Tuck and Roll 6:58

TOTAL TIME 69:21

JACK VAD Recording Engineer
HAL SOOGIAN Sound Engineer
KIRK SCHREIL Audio Crew
LISA WOODWARD Audio Crew

THANKS TO THESE PUBLISHERS
Boosey & Hawkes, Inc. (Del Tredici, Mackey)
Peer Classical (Harrison)
C.F. Peters (Cage, Feldman, Ives: ©1962 by C.F. Peters Corp. Used by permission)
G. Schirmer, Inc. (Antheil, Cowell)

Mackey recording courtesy of The RCA Victor Group, A Unit of BMG Entertainment. All other performances recorded live during the American Mavericks festival, June 2000. See program listings, page 120, for performers.